how architecture got its hump

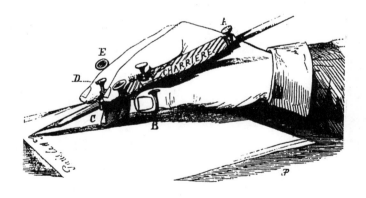

Charrière, a device designed to counter the problem of writer's cramp.
Drawing from *L'Arsenale de la chirurgie* (Paris: G. Gaujot, 1867).

how architecture got its hump ROGER CONNAH

Preston Thomas Memorial Lecture Series
Department of Architecture
Cornell University, Ithaca, New York

The MIT Press
Cambridge, Massachusetts
London, England

This book was set in Garamond by Achorn Graphic Services, Inc.

Printed and bound in the United States of America.

Library of Congress Cataloging-in-Publication Data
Connah, Roger.
    How architecture got its hump / Roger Connah.
      p. cm.
    Includes bibliographical references and index.
    ISBN 0-262-53188-7 (pbk.: alk. paper)
    1. Architecture—Philosophy. I. Title.
NA2500.C596 2001
720′.1—dc21
                                                    00-064595

to John Hejduk, 1929–2000

for his passion and encouragement,
a far cry from architecture as we think we know it

To live in the modern world is to live

in what is clearly a bardo ream:

you don't have to die to experience one.

—SOGYAL RINPOCHE, *The Tibetan Book of Living and Dying*

. . . a bull is an apparent congruity, and real incongruity, of ideas, suddenly discovered. . . . [T]he pleasure arising from wit proceeds from our surprise at suddenly discovering two things to be similar, in which we suspected no similarity. The pleasure arising from bulls proceeds from our discovering two things to be dissimilar, in which a resemblance might have been suspected.

—SYDNEY SMITH, *Works*

And the Camel humphed himself, humph and all, and went away to join the Three. And from that day to this the Camel always wears a humph (we call it "hump" now, not to hurt his feelings); but he has never yet caught up with the three days that he missed at the beginning of the world, and he has never yet learned how to behave.

—RUDYARD KIPLING, *"How the Camel Got His Hump"*

contents

acknowledgments

"No matter how much you squeeze a handful of sand," a Tibetan saying has it, "you will never get oil out of it." I always feel, and this is not a bad thing, that we are always in the middle of ongoing conversations. This book began as a series of four lectures called "Mind the Gap," delivered as the Preston Thomas Memorial Lectures at Cornell University in 1995. The lectures were sketched choreographically. Ideas built up, commented, and echoed other ideas as allusions, references, and specific or chance "stories" were picked up. Just as in architecture today, this might be more easily described as a memetic approach. I would like to thank Mrs. Ruth Thomas for the opportunity to use the Preston Thomas Memorial Lectures to develop these ideas in an unconventional way. More Little Prince than Vers Une Architecture, more innumerable low-lying skerries than a thousand plateaus, I have tried to retain the same tenor in the essays as in the lectures. The provocative and impossible skerries that architecture has nothing to do with communication (the self-canceling seductions of meaning and style) and an architecture dispersing a much rawer power are issues the lectures discussed and the essays resonate. But in the book, as in the lectures, I have preferred to avoid the membership and organized narrative around the tacit "star community" of contemporary architects. By so doing I hope to suggest that those architects producing apparently quite different architectures might really be dealing with similar issues. Thus, I also chose to avoid showing spectacular slides of buildings, unusual details, and other seductive moments in architecture. Instead, not so much as to deny the seduction of these buildings in a visual sense, this offered an opportunity to show more fragile, less predetermined, even surprising departures for architectural issue. That is why accompanying the essays there are examples of scribbles, drawings, doodles, lines, and calligraphic exercises selected from, among others, Kipling, St. Exupéry, Sterne, Stendhal, and Barthes.* My thanks must also go to Professor John Miller for his continued support and interest in the lectures, Amy Cash for her hospitality at Cornell University, and the students for picking up on the choreography of the lectures. A shorter version of the fourth lecture, "Archobabble," was delivered at the Anyway event in Barcelona in 1993, while the first lecture was aired as an opening to a festival on film and architecture, hosted by the Arkitektur Centrum, in Vienna in 1995. My thanks go to Cynthia Davidson and Dietmar Steiner, respectively, for these two events.

Helsinki, Stockholm, and Ruthin, North Wales

* *Editor's note:* The author has made every effort to trace the copyright holders, but if he has inadvertently overlooked any, he will be pleased to make the necessary arrangement at the first opportunity.

introduction mind the gap

I know those little phrases that seem so innocuous, and, once you let them in, pollute the whole of speech. "Nothing is more real than nothing." They rise up out of the pit and know no rest until they drag you down into its dark.

—SAMUEL BECKETT[1]

Who tells architecture to walk? Who tells architecture to pause? Who tells architecture to stop at the edge? When stepping onto London Underground trains a voice announces, "Mind the gap!" The voice is usually indifferent, unconcerned, and routine. Most visitors to London will remember this voice.

The warning is about the gap between the edge of the Underground platform and the train itself. To avoid falling into that gap—the void—it is necessary to take a more than usual step. Hence the stern, recorded voice says, "Mind the gap!" In a brief text called *Architecture and the Pathognomic* (1991), John Hejduk wrote about an architectural disease and the pathological signs of architecture's current wound. Architecture had suddenly developed a hump, symptoms of which, Hejduk felt, were "hidden under the appearance of a still-functioning organism." To go by the turn-of-the-millennium mediation, architecture certainly still appears to be functioning, but it was the activity of the "continued" presence of a disease that concerned Hejduk. It was a hump also that architecture might have had for much longer than imagined. Under these diseased conditions, the workers within the discipline, hardly in overalls or grease stained, are forced to define their operational stand. Hejduk listed the options:

1. To totally ignore the situation and go about their business as if nothing has changed.
2. To do research and take an active part in combatting the disease through the "exploration and searching" for a cure and the hopeful eventual eradication of the potentially dead bacteria.
3. To gently help the discipline through its death and wait for a "rebirth," the form, structure, and content of which is yet to come.[2]

The development of architecture has for some time now proceeded on an interactive gaming between persona and dis-

course, theory and praxis, discipline and interference, fame and
production. It has become, if not been for a long time, memetic. Trying to reduce detail about this or that architect or this
or that building might allow us to share ideas, sensibilities,
expectations—even exaggerations—about architecture, but it
also tends to encourage us to occupy genres and critical camps
far too hastily. Contemporary journals do their best to fuse
fashion with architecture, truly a meme machine,[3] but it
should not disguise a grander indifference to fashion itself. Architects can discover that their beloved realm is about "space"
or "place" all over again and announce it in an incomplete,
dazzling rhetoric—a rhetorical flourish that often appears to
demonstrate little or no awareness of critical repetition or difference. In critical history, a growing thinness and confusion
continues warning us that visual dissimilarity should never disguise mutual quest. Theoretical similarity does not necessarily
engender similar visual compulsion.

Architecture has and will always be subject to interrelations
with other disciplines. Film, photography, drawing, philosophy, and language are perhaps more familiar and fashionable
interferences. Recent indications suggest that dance, music,
opera, physics, chaos theories, the new science of materials,
computer science and software, and even boxing and cuisine
are now being explored as serious analogical sources and interference for architectural theory, production, space, and metaphysics. It is not always clear how or why these interferences
have appeared and whether they have "humped" architecture
into an irreversible hybrid activity. However, it is clear that
other disciplines have begun informing architecture at a time
when architecture itself appears most fragile, most open, most

wounded, that is, when the pathology has begun to set in. So strong has been the intertextual traffic and interdisciplinarity, the last thirty years have seen architecture not only scaffolded by disciplines beyond its considered domain but further destabilized, delimited or—to use a more topical term—deterritorialized. If so, and warned by Hejduk, are we not forced to ask the question: Is it only in a movement between something essential and something redundant that we can begin to see what these various disciplines might have brought, and continue to bring, to architecture?

Film and architecture? Photography and architecture? Drawing and architecture? Language and architecture? Philosophy and architecture? Criticism and architecture? It is unclear whether these interferences are mere props for scenographic lift, which architects so badly warn themselves against, or departures for a serious architectural production so urgently sought in our contemporary hybridity. These interferences may even offer serious alibis for an architecture we can as yet not recognize. Were we fond of neologisms, we might invent a "superstructuralism" or "transstructuralism" for an architecture ignored by all other names! Would this be a hybrid scenario continually oscillating and reinventing classical and Renaissance moves? Or are we faced with something more fluid, an architecture with a future, a permanent unrest, an architectural hell of our own making? Does this not invite us now, more than ever, to reassess that useful condition of the unnecessary that goes by the term *redundancy?*

Having no clear idea how or why architecture needs these scaffolding disciplines does not alter a potentially irreversible development. Should we be content observing how architecture bounces off, and is bounced off, these different disciplines? Much has been claimed about how disciplines inform and alter each other through relations that are usually asymmetric. These disciplines can lean toward or then swerve away from each other. It is no longer impossible to extend this and think of opera and architecture, football and architecture, fashion and architecture, cuisine and architecture, electronics and architecture, Buddhism and architecture, gardening and architecture, Lego and architecture, dance and architecture, memetics and architecture . . .

"Mind the gap" serves as a useful metaphor, albeit disposable after the journey, for the informing, interactive, and interfering relationships between various disciplines and architecture. Film is not architecture. Architecture is not film. Drawing is not architecture. Architecture is not drawing. Nor is architecture photography, philosophy, Lego, or Sufism. Though these disciplines may appear parallel, if not "bullishly" redundant in relation to each other, judging by the increase in discursive activity, their support, symbiosis, and synergy grows by the nanosecond.

Architecture waits! Like an Underground station, it waits until film, dance, philosophy, chaos theory, Sufism, or the geometry of nature arrives. Some Underground stations in London are old, dark, historical, dirty, and full of graffiti! Others are freshly planned, imaginatively designed, light, and—full of graffiti! Upon the train's arrival we hear the warning that is also an option: "Mind the gap!" We can step onto the train and travel. We can entertain film, drawing, photography, opera (or whatever) as a helpful discipline, prod, alibi, or interference. We can alight at the next station after a brief trip. Or then we can remain onboard. What happens if we remain traveling?

Architecture waits! In London and Glasgow it is possible to take a round-trip, in which case the journey would be infinite. Each time arriving at another station, another architecture, another discipline, another interference, another voice announces, "Mind the gap." In the infinity that results as one leans into the other, Jean-Luc Godard's words come to mind: "Le moral? C'est le traveling." The lightness of this traveling, of course, has never ever been as casual as it may seem. We could naturally not do anything like this. We could merely let the train come into the station, wave to those within, and then allow it to leave without getting on. However, architecture would then not be prevented from being what it already is!

₁ **move, every still moment!** *on film and architecture*

The immense volume of open space that separated the building from the neighbouring high-rise a quarter of a mile away un-settled his sense of balance. At times he felt that he was living in the gondola of a ferris wheel permanently suspended three hundred feet above ground.

—J. G. BALLARD [1]

Film and architecture! Immediate qualifications allowing us to gloss this pairing come to mind: "film" in architecture, "filming" architecture, "filmic" architecture. Immediate loose assumptions follow. In the first, film informs the theoretical discourses in architecture. In the second, a more pragmatic move, film actually "films" architecture. The third, the cinematic act, is a poetics. This is an interpretive gesture, a critical stance, aiding or abetting architectural tectonics and hermeneutics. In our reflections, it is this latter that we will consider here. In the spread (the smear?) of one discipline across another, we will confine ourselves to the way film has been seen to, or is consistently assumed to, inform, interact, and interfere with architecture.

We might voice an immediate fear: Have we already missed the train? In our theoretical concern are we about to rewrite and reformulate what Bernard Tschumi already did in the *Manhattan Transcripts?* Are we to use film, as Tschumi suggested, as a transcription *of a random accumulation of events,* thereby co-opting, coercing, and then willing these events—global, metropolitan, urban, or suburban—into new, unrecognized architectonic organizations? Just what does a "cumulative event" mean in architecture? Could this be an alibi for the wider promise of ephemeral architecture? And what of an "eventful" architecture?[2] Are we not faced with architectural events that go in and out of sense, just as in literature or poetry we oscillate daily between the sense and nonsense we can make of our own worlds and environments?

To speak then of film and architecture might also be to hold to Jacques Derrida's aphorism: "These assertions only make sense in the condition of an analogy between discourse and all the so-called arts of space."[3] Might we not gain more by appropriately restricting ourselves to film's attractive, and often more pragmatically confused, hold on architectural production? We would thus be occupied by exploring only the hijack of film by architecure. By no means a recent concern, film has for much of this century in one form or another knocked on architecture's door. And though earlier in the century, film or film studies might not have been referred to directly, the very ubiquitous poetics of the "motion" picture could not have failed to inform, distract, and interfere with many earlier architects.

We recall Le Corbusier's cinematic statement: "Arab architecture has much to teach us. It is appreciated while on the move, with one's feet. . . . [I]t is while walking, moving from one place to another, that one sees how the arrangements of the architecture develop." An architecture appreciated while on the move leans on scenography as much as scripting. More revealingly Le Corbusier's statement asks us to consider how ambiguous and interrelated have been the relationships between two of the strongest aesthetic metaphors of modernism: scene and screen. Following Le Corbusier's prompt, architecture became a script for the movement of the observer.[4]

Accepting the ambiguity of Le Corbusier's *real* architectural promenade, a scripted architecture in motion takes over from painting which, according to Sergei Eisenstein, remained incapable of fixing the total representation of a phenomenon in its full visual multiplicity. We need only recall other words of Eisenstein to go beyond Eisenstein himself, for what, indeed, besides film has proved capable of a phenomenology revealing full visual multiplicity. "Only the film camera has solved the problem of doing this on a flat surface," Eisenstein claims, "but its undoubted ancestor in this capability is architecture." Fast-forward this to the endless stream of tortuous reasoning and poststructuralist encounters at the end of the twentieth century and we begin to see how the exploration of movement and unrest has turned into an inevitable poetics of architectural disquiet. Rewrite the following Gilles Deleuze's script for film, with architecture infiltrating through the seams, and we can see the arrival that is so often deferred today: "The any-instant-whatever is the instant which is equidistant from another. We can therefore define cinema [architecture] as the system which reproduces movement by relating it to the 'any-instant-whatever.'" Occasionally achieved with subtlety, more often with aching, even mindless, thinness, as Ignasi de Solà-Morales reminds us, "A certain fashion, first in Europe and then in America, has seized upon the dazzling images of his [Deleuze's] thought, either as forms to be directly visualized in new architectures or as verbal metaphors with which to beautify a conventional, if not vulgar, way of thinking."[5]

Anywhere you look, in any book on media and cultural studies, or film theory and criticism, sentences like the following will appear open to architectural hijack: "Here there are no ethical values, no pure states: everything is destined to emerge, develop, and die within this movement."[6] Whether we can fast-forward such poetics of unrest to the claims made for an architecture without any pure state, with no ethical values, we should leave on the back burner. It would, however, be useful to remember Adorno while recalling Tschumi's words on fireworks: "Good architecture must be conceived, erected and burned in vain. The greatest architecture of all is the fireworker's: it perfectly shows the gratuitous consumption of pleasure."[7]

It may also perfectly fizzle out. Obviously as a celestial notation, fireworks are hardly redundant, though gratuitous they may be to the more conventional architectural evidence expected elsewhere.

If we return to the pathology of the gap, we may find John Hejduk right all along to warn us not only of the systems of collapse in architecture but the implied inversions, the systems of healing, the misunderstood backlash of resistance. "Eliminate the word *systems*," Hejduk concludes, "and retain the illumination of collapse—healing-death-rebirth."[8] To retain the illumination of collapse, to salute architecture's redundancy, to recall our ancestors and yet to remain in hope of an ethical drive—we are in good company. In this way can we not speak of film against architecture? Or might film be to architecture as a good tango couple, helping us to suspect, inspect, and interrogate the politics of everyday life?

"I once went looking for locations in India with a man who had worked as an art director for Terry Gilliam. I realised that for Terry to make a film he first had to build a city." The director Stephen Frears felt he didn't need to build a city; he could just turn up on the street with a camera and the people would form themselves into expressive patterns: "I could in other words make up the film as I went along and that gave my work, I thought, a lot of its vitality. But the other day, on the phone with Terry I found myself saying with some embarrassment that I had begun to discover the joy of approaching a film as a series of images as well as a story."[9] Is this a grand innocence or has Stephen Frears, like many, been looking the wrong way for so many years? Approaching a film as a series of images as well as a story! Many architects have attempted the reverse for the last twenty or thirty years, trying to discover the joy of approaching architecture as a story instead of a series of images, as an event instead of anything remotely connected to dwelling. Whether such reversals have succeeded probably depends not only on the way we see, read, and experience many of the newer architectural projects, but how we read the "story" they try to tell or the communication they resist.[10]

The poetics of fireworks invites obvious questions within our remit: Is film redundant to architecture? Is film leaning on architecture only to see architecture hijacking film? Are they perhaps not only strangers and enigmas to themselves but parasites? Before we try to lay out a few guidelines and options for our study of the architectural hijack, there is a perfect reply to the question of the useful "redundancy" of fireworks. Such condition of the unnecessary is to be found in Paul Auster's novel *The Music of Chance:*

He never wanted to do that again, he realized, but once he left the town behind him and could accelerate on the empty road, it was hard not to pretend for a little while, to imagine that he was back in those days before the real story of his life had begun. This was the only chance he would have, and he wanted to savor what had been given to him, to push the memory of who he had once been as far as it would go.[11]

   While respecting much that passed in the twentieth century for more than the scenographic fraud played on us, there is now an urgent, clear, and uncompromising desire to push the memory of architecture as it *once* was as far as it *now* can go. Film refuses to let go. Like any alibi, scaffolded reason or motive, film can redefine architecture, derail it for a time, or then merely travel alongside. The dangers are self-evident. Like good research, they depend upon what we set out to find. If, when we marry film and architecture, we seek a partial totality, then we can certainly build a case for such achievement. If we prefer "to make more sense," or indeed think we can "make more sense," we might speak of an architecture complete with missing parts.

   Make sense who may, this too offers itself to our gaze and interpretation. By allowing for such approaches we may find much contemporary architecture offering witness of a type of building we cannot readily assimilate or even accommodate. A bull in literary usage is a statement that can appear paradoxical at the same time as offering some sense. Though of unknown origin, in Old French, *boul* is "fraud," "deceit," "trickery." In Middle English, *bull* is "falsehood." It can never be too far away from the Icelandic *bull,* which is "nonsense." The architectural "bull"—that creative incongruity Sydney Smith describes—might be in advance of itself, in advance of the partial architectures it always manages to erase before completion. Accepting this, though, it might even be possible to offer some credibility to newer, errant architectures, architectures ambushed by their own surprise and unrest, without the cynicism of known voodoo and borrowed theory.

Onboard a Delta Airlines flight from San Francisco to London, on the in-flight entertainment video was a program called *The Know-Zone*. The future of the great outdoors seemed indoors at thirty-eight thouand feet. Mobile homes were about to become motor coaches fitted with virtual reality screens and screams. No one could hear their neighbors anymore. As if computers invented the crysallis, a house like a butterfly was presented, while the most ecologically correct house was made from recycled motor car tires. A "Kitchen 2000" was so intelligent that tampering with added garlic and honey yogurt in Genovese pesto looked decidedly amateur. The high-tech cooking island owed a lot to film-set design, while the holographic projection controlled the command center of the vegetable section. The climate-controlled electronic pantry looked as tasty as a fountain pen display in Harrods, and if you ventured to take anything from the two-sided cylindrical fridge, then beware the curtain of gruesome, healthy air! Washing, water, and solids made the microprocessing simple. The only thing left for the cynic before curling up in fetal simulation and making stoutness exercises loaned from Pooh Bear was a little, hitherto unknown idea called digital enhancement, which was about to become a well-known idea called Digital Enhancement!

The dream house drawn by Dream House Wisher looked a lot like Frank Lloyd Wright, run, as it would be, by a director who would prefer the house to have a little more "power plant" rhetoric and *Brazil* narrative. Oh, the joy of a series of images without any story! The director as architect proved redundant, as the house was then taken over by a solar-run computer. This smart house needed no one around, not even the simulated guard dog. There was no "Help" button, no further justification for ideas, as redundancy had already reached this far in the eradicaton of architecture in the infallible future.

Yet how does architecture seek the support and justification for its ideas? As architecture visits other disciplines, as it hijacks philosophy, as it surfs with Heidegger and Benjamin and ransacks Derrida or Deleuze for the dazzle of metaphor, architecture looks as if it needs expanding and containing at the same time.[12] Should we warn ourselves immediately against the predictability of these crossover disciplines, film and architecture? When both disciplines cannibalize the other, is nothing but a shadow syntax left? We may no longer be able to detach ourselves from a fashionable application of film in architecture; we may be memetically controlled to be seduced. When film theory, when phenomenology, postmodernism, deconstruction, chaos theory, and computer software become fodder for architectural production, is there still a need for any safety valve?

Clever, innovative applications of such material and sources feed architectural progress. Lesser experiments make from this source a form of circus vernacularism, unethical theme parks, tacky film sets, cut-out architectural theater, all of which doubtless feeds the already desolate architectural market.

Supported by critical language, indecipherability becomes hip. Supported by very little language at all, invisibility becomes hype. Film vocabulary has already redefined architecture as fast as structural paradigms are left behind. And though architecture read through the vocabulary and discourse of film studies is part of critical and interpretive studies, I would suggest that this is of less relevance here unless the option is offered in which film begins to "read" architecture anew.

Meaning and interpretations that cross over from film to architecture may begin to come up with validities that are sustainable.[13] Interactivity and interference between film and architecture might then not only correspond to the collective material the world offers us, but take us beyond these into the privatized sphere. Here the novels of J. G. Ballard or Philip K. Dick have already done more to warn us of and prepare us for the "gap" than the cyberpunks. As Douglas Rushkoff puts it:

Similarly the art and literature of Cyberia have abandoned the clear lines and smooth surfaces of *Star Trek* and *2001: A Space Odyssey* in favour of the grimy post-urban realism of *Batman, Neuromancer* and *Blade Runner,* in which computers do not simplify human issues but expose and even amplify the obvious faults in our systems of logic and social engineering.[14]

If architecture can be as personal and redundant as any filmed dream or dreamed film, there may be one obvious consequence. This is a *provisional architecture* setting up its own corrective strategy for every moment, every accumulation of events, and every eventuality—earthquake or war, terror or heat wave, Sarajevo or Seoul, Oklahoma, Atlanta, Belfast, or Pristina. This is as an architecture that dissolves its own determination, that resists the stability of events and resists any nameable movement, opting too for the instability of any information, all critical access denied. A monstrous existence?

Perhaps. Yet the most obvious and surprising use film can be to architecture might be as an essential *and* unnecessary operational motive, just as Lebbeus Woods asks of us to "draw architecture as though it were already built." This is a "redundant" operation, a myth for the architectural process, the use of fireworks to map out architectural maneuvers in the sky. Here film would operate as a clue. As in a detective story, we are well aware that there are ultimately no redundant clues. We know, too, that only some of the clues are essential to resolve the mystery. Similarly in any architectural narrative. "Imagine," Woods continues, "that it has in this way been freed of its original purposes, those that once justified its existence, but no longer can."

So much analytical work was produced on language, linguistics, and sign theory between 1930 and 1960 that it was inevitable that such research would not remain closeted in linguistics itself. In architecture, the understanding of the role of sign and the strategies of communication logic have since probably been influenced more by journalism, film reviewing, and fashion writing than the more scholarly attempts to locate architecture's arrested significance. And certainly, much has been claimed for the apparent democratization of sign over the past twenty or thirty years. The public access to architecture through a sign system was, however, doomed from the beginning. Its claims were bound to be compromised by the looseness of language itself.[15]

Language continually invites architecture to slip into a redundancy through its own totalizing power, referred to by Frank Heron as "the upset of the cerebral."[16] Hopelessly lost, this allows the currency of the fragment(ary) in meaning as well as in architecture. Wanting to engage and yet disengage at the time same time is a serious irresponsibility that film shares with architecture, just as architecture was to take on its cosmo-genetic traces in the 1990s to explain this "upset of the cerebral."[17] An example from Charles Jencks's newer language will illustrate the slide into inevitable approximation: "Some of the most beautiful architectural compositions in the world emerge precisely from the juxtaposition of very different styles clearly and courageously relating through time."[18] The operative words here are not "juxtaposition" or "very different styles," for they merely open the critical floodgates to include all. The controlling words here—and they have become the tacit moral condition of recognizing good architecture by some and not others—are the words "clearly and courageously." The clear and courageous building of symbol, disaster, or organic hysteria that relate through time is language so close to being meaningless that we must address this as some sort of "fashionable nonsense" and semiotic catastrophe.[19]

What, then, might film have lent to the architectural sign? What has it still to lend in this continual oscillation between discipline and desire? In the late twentieth century, much unthinking hybridization in architecture resulted from what can be seen now as a facile, literal scenography. A well-meaning desire to read architecture as a subset of language left us with the obvious ambiguity; "reading" architecture became a fetish of coded responses and armed codes. Architecture attempted to produce medial facades, holographic memories on the surface of the street. Symbolism was flattened to a public-access architecture. Form became braille, and the ontic and ontological were metaphysical game plans for architecture operating according to a simple and simplistic mechanics. Architecture showed itself open to inevitable aesthetic management and displacement, with ethics left forlorn. It began to inform and deform itself with the will of images and the will to image. This led to architectures of the sign of the sign. It was a "welcome to echo-world!"—cancel-out time. In our Circle Line metaphor, the Underground train was arriving at the station but not stopping, because of a black bag lying at the steps of the exit staircase—because of a bomb alert!

Is it reasonable to speak in such a way of the hijack of film by architecture? If there is a continuous anxiety of influence and interference between film and architecture could it not also open up quite remarkable areas? Apart from keeping architecture controlled by familiar scenography, different, unassimilable architectures could result—architecture that might not only be beyond present theory but, more fortunately and teasingly, beyond eventual documentation. For purposes of inquiry, we will look at how four interferences, four approaches between film and architecture respond to four types of thinking-out and thinking-through architecture. Importantly, these approaches do not always collide with the ways of reading architecture. Hence, within this gap, between production and interpretation, lies the redundant hope possible in contemporary architecture, particularly in the unassimilable. Within these four approaches, some of this thinking has already produced serious architectural experience. There is, however, nothing linear about these visions. They obviously loan, borrow from, and cannibalize each other. To say this is nothing new. Architecture has always been cannibalistic, and may—with the language available—be irreversibly memetic!

A "lift" from Godard again proves useful for us here: "Of course architecture can have beginnings, middles and ends. But not necessarily in that order." If film theory gives us nothing else, if we merely stumble upon architecture of someone else's meaning, or random clichés and maxims about discontinuity, this upset surely would be enough. We will call these four visions: literal architectures, nomadic architectures, undressed architectures and private architectures. They are named after their approach to thinking, not their sylistic membership. All of these visions—some more theoretical than others—can use film as an architectural prop. This is not the point. The point is how they are aware of, how they operate in, and how they "Mind the gap!" And for one who knew more of the "gap" than most in the past century, the warning is there. "There are people," Levi-Strauss put it, "who wring their hands and call it an abyss, but do nothing to fill it; there are also those who work to widen it . . ." We should update this with our contemporary passion for unrest: there are also those who work and travel within it. We would hope architectural visions such as these, too, are aware of the traveling. To echo Federico García Lorca: although architecture may know the roads, it may never arrive at Cordoba!

Literal Architectures

First, the so-called straight application of film to architecture, if indeed anything "straight" is possible today in such coded-anti-coded conditions. This is what we could call literal architectures, usefully described here, in relation to film at least, as the metropolis factor.[20] Filmic composition and scenography operate as literal signifiers for the architectural program. Architectural production can then shadow this program or divert it with yet other agendas, resulting in a cinematics of architecture. Strongly visual, it can be residual, urban, metropolitan, or utopian. There are many relevant, popular models from film for such scenographic hijack.[21]

Briefly, the films of Fritz Lang, Ridley Scott, and Terry Gilliam, for example, tempt an architecture of spectacle where significance, through its visual seduction, struggles to survive its literalness. The films of, say, Robert Bresson, Michelangelo Antonioni, and Wim Wenders treat this seduction differently. They suggest an architecture of economy in which significance is pointed up by visual emphasis. The excess of both approaches depends on how much is required from the discreet composition within architecture, and how much seduction is allowable in the grand scene. In other words, it depends how the program from film is converted into the production of architecture.

Take the section in *The Fisher King* (directed by Terry Gilliam), where Grand Central Station turns into a whirling choreographic stage. Compare this to the long opening of Wenders's *Paris, Texas,* where Harry Dean Stanton walks from being a dot on the landscape to main man. To put this in a more familiar architectural way of seeing, we can consider this as Frank Lloyd Wright of the Hollyhock House compared with Mies van der Rohe of the Barcelona Pavilion. In film terms, Wright dissolves some of his details one to the other; no one is quite sure where symbol ends and sign begins. Mies van der Rohe, however, attempts more subtlety. His treatment of space cuts the shot abruptly. This "dissolve" (continuity) and/or the length of the "cut" (discontinuity) correspond to different ways of structuring architectural events, leading clearly to different ways to offer experience and invite perception.

If we were to try to put this distinction between dissolve and cut in a deeper critical jargon from cinema, we could follow Seymour Chatman on Antonioni, who speaks of "the surface of the event versus the event of the surface."[22] As a literal signification and application into architecture, such poetics usually co-opt the surface of the screen and remain weakly scenographic. This was the case with much postmodernism, as its early semantic interrogation was flattened and carnivalized into weak memetically produced repertoires in the 1980s. Responding to markets of the architectural sign, postmodern architecture quickly began to feed its own signals. Seduction was uppermost and often left the obvious—a potential architectural performance and unrest trapped in a somewhat predictable theatricality. Many now agree, apart from the unique projects which triggered the movement in general, that postmodernism produced an architectural semantic theatricality we are no longer stunned by, nor even fascinated by.

The blame is not merely on postmodernism, however, nor the fetish theories snacked on like cocktail sausages pricked with toothpicks that eventually get up the nose. The same happens when the provocative or dazzling image-thinking of those like Maurice Blanchot, Edmond Jabès, Derrida, Deleuze, and Fernando Pessoa are squeezed back into architectural production. The phenomenology of diaspora, backlash, and collapse always leaves lesser architecture an eventual prop for applicable theories and fashionable metaphors. We must remain true to the exception.

Where theory is consumed faster than anthologies can collate its transformations as architecture, a confusion arises. In the case of *literal architectures,* this is the confusion between an architecture of cinema and the cinema of architecture. The result is an iconic hijack. If we could rely on this passing quickly and quietly, we might be unconcerned about its current status. But it must be acolwledged. It does look as if some cultures will remain obsessed with the facile concern for an architecture of iconic effect. In terms of architecture as the patient, this is a facial lift.[23]

Dangerously, this iconic hijack can begin to operate as a normative myth for architecture. It allows little regeneration, ensuring perpetuity only in an architectural hope of changing imagery and pixelated phantoms long drifting away. It plays games of logic and reason with its own chosen past. Architecture as a tummy tuck or a chin tuck, as the plastic surgeons call them. If, however, such a normative myth and pull do take over, might not serious inquiry be given to the extent to which these architectures *are* medial facades or—like certain cancers—irremedial events? Perhaps this is a concern already co-opted more by Paul Virilio's project than Venturi's "approach to the facade as a manifestation of urban context and an example of evolving Classicism." The latter is a semantic strategy which, Venturi felt, justified the National Gallery project and acts as an apologia for their work in general.[24]

When Virilio speaks of the "surface becoming the interactive depth," he does not merely mean more enticing screens on buildings, nor only a manifestation of urban context. That would be merely a replication of the electronic scenography, hijacking Venturi's earlier attempts to take this on in his Hall of Fame in New Brunswick in 1967. This was the type of televisual display we saw exploited so well by Nike's advertisement for the 1994 World Cup in soccer, which had Eric Cantona kicking the ball to Romario and Bebeto, only to be saved by the gaily colored, acrobatic Mexican goalkeeper Campos, in some dislocated scenography resembling a cross between *Blade Runner* and the Ennis Brown House.[25]

To be fair, much contemporary work and thinking have already begun liberating architecture from this iconic concern. Venturi's role in this has been ungenerously underplayed by critics preferring to condemn him for semantic inanity rather than his more ambiguous achievement to liberate the pixel. But here it is the "scene" itself, not the "screen," that is being redefined. Nowhere better can this delicacy be seen than in the strong architectural work carried out by Jacques Herzog and Pierre de Meuron. Surface of the event or the event of the surface, but for these architects, like Toyo Ito, film is just one of the techniques that modern media provide for architecture. Mass, imagery, structure, material, and light all combine to reverse the screen and scene. Abstraction is redefined by the ordinariness of their work in its context. If the images are literal and even disembodied in television and film, in architecture an evident materiality offers tactility and sublimation.

Solà-Morales categorizes this as a process of reestablishing the principles of architecture that seem as remote from modern efficiency as they are from postmodern historical memory:

In many of their buildings, the meaning is established by neither the context nor the tectonicity, nor the sense of the place or the typological or figurative references to other architectures of the past. They do not intend such remembrance to be the way of their affirmation. Their architecture is, in some degree, much more immediate and direct; it can be perceived through the kinaesthetic experience of those who look at it.[26]

An architecture ultimately far from the ordinary? "In Hitchcock movies," Herzog says, "everything is so normal; then suddenly there is depth. Even normal things can be new." This is the David Lynch world transferred to a Europe of Swatch and Benetton surface worlds and carnivalized as quickly as you can say "catwalk," by fashion itself. Support taking the form of a "literal" metaphor (in terms of thinness) becomes an index of activity. It offers the narrative event of film as a sketch for the normative scheme, but falls short of defining a waywardly different poetics for architecture. Entering pragmatic architectural conversation, we get a sort of precyberspace gossip about fantastic sets, crystal mazes, and virtual reality.

Twin Peaks, for example, was fashionable in all suburbs of the globe because it was fashioned for peak viewing, peak attention. A fetish surrealism, it employed about seven or eight narratives within an alterable chess-game/word-processing structure that allows any director to visit for less than a minute. These narratives continually came around, like the characters

Audrey, Shelly, and Donna filmed tantalizingly, as in a rotis-serie. Everything was held together by the architect, hard-hat Agent Cooper, apple pie, damn fine coffee, and an extraordi-nary cinema craft applied on the televisual scale. With a bit of luck, David Lynch and Mark Frost summed up the twentieth-century's genres, thereby allowing cinema to get on with newer unexpected forms in this century.

Knowing that perception can be altered by electronic media more than the sparkle of pixels offers a more immediate archi-tectural tool. In the work of Herzog and de Meuron, sceno-graphic versions of screens in the environment look likely to give way to serious questions of the screen in architecture, a direction Venturi looked like he was heading in before re-maining within the evolved and evolving facade. Altering scenography suggests Alfred Hitchcock, Ray Bradbury, or Philip K. Dick. Interrogating screens within architectural space itself suggest the networks and cyberspace of William Gibson and the more emerging "literary" departure for such architecture. Let us not, however, write off too hastily further architectural thrill from this, but offer a simple summary of the visual options for literal architectures: the film *Blade Runner* or William Gibson's novel *Neuromancer*? Viva the electronic aesthetic—over the ma-chine aesthetic? "We are not," Herzog has said, "architects who wake up in the morning and know what we're going to do."[27]

Nomadic Architectures

The second interference and interplay between architecture and film involves the self-reflexive act. This is the questioning of the soul in front of the mirror, the screen. This project not only involves a radical questioning of the theory of applying film to architecture, but sees this as an architectural project resolving itself through its own discursive involvement and movement. The program of film responds to and within the production of architecture. In other words, instead of loosely applying Husserlian, Derridean, or Heideggerean ideas to architecture, such an architectural program begins to question the unstable relevance of such ideas (and of course the relevance of instability itelf). This project finds an echo in the earlier notion of redundancy, also clearly echoed in Gilles Deleuze, especially in his book *Cinema 1: The Movement-Image* (1986).

Architecture may share with film the pull on any story it tries to achieve. Due to editing and less to linear narrative, architecture naturally takes its own drama from montage rather than anecdote. To take off from here we need to return to Eisenstein: "At the basis of the composition of the architectural ensemble . . . lies that same unique *dance* which is the basis of the creation of works of music, painting and film montage."[28] That same unique dance? To simplify this we will speak of the way montage can occur within the frame (the way the frame is assembled) and the way montage can also occur between frames. The latter as an operation takes us from one event to another, whether in a film cut, or a "cut" in an architectural sequence. There is no longer any strangeness in utilizing such vocabulary or such devices so central has such an operation become to understand the assemblage of architecture.[29] On the move, the cut is either abrupt or gradual. We dissolve from the plane of the feasible into the plane of the unfeasible. Sense and non-sense collide until we make an order from them. "Get into the scene late," as David Mamet says, "get out of the scene early, tell the story in the cut."[30] Understanding this would bring us nearer to understanding a building such as Daniel Libeskind's Jewish Museum Extension in Berlin, or some of his later works. In flight, such architecture is then seen as disquiet. Gently or not as the case may be, it upsets more than the cerebral. It upsets the *axis mundi*.

"It's important to remember," Mamet continues, "that it is not the dramatist's [architect's] task to create confrontation or chaos but, rather, to create order. Start with the disordering event, and let the beat be about the attempt to restore order."[31] Of course this radical-montage thinking has less power when it is reduced to a replication of architectonic devices and rhetorical moves seen in architectural magazines throughout the world. These are strange times when tilts can suggest order and dislocation locks out the silence of its own energy. So common are such moves (memes?) that it has become easy to attack the tame and the thin: "Aren't we tired of our subjection to boring esoterica promoting arconcepture involving cuckoo sculptural form defined by old-fashioned shadow and archaic engineering which is really decoration?"[32]

The idea of a "radical montage" is possibly at an early stage in architecture. If, as Thomas Pynchon describes in *Gravity's Rainbow,* both film and calculus are pornographies of flight, could it not also be a warning to ourselves? A radical montage in architecture growing into another pornography of flight and in flight? Speaking of flight and "minding the gap," the work of Deleuze again comes to mind: "On the one hand, you can bring two instants or two positions together to infinity; but movement will always occur in the interval between the two.

In other words behind your back"[33]—in other words, ideas
and events, theories and sequences not laid out with unalter-
able guidelines but sneaking up on you, behind your back.
Architecture, like cinema, is not an image to which movement
is added. Instead, it is a production that is intervened with
and interfered with; it offers an up-and-running movement-
image and becomes an architecture happening behind your
back. Not only still images but still, images. This is an architecture not really wanting to know what is going to happen
anymore. "Imaging" itself beyond the feasible, this is an architecture not content with predisposition and prescription, but
an architecture ambushed by its own movement. In more direct terms, architecture translates itself from a building entered
to one passed through, bypassed, architectonically, from the
fluid tectonics of a building like the Carpenter Centre to a
dream of movement in continuity—hijacked flight!

Search any of Bernard Tschumi's language about architecture's hopes and you will find these dreams reinterpreting and
repeating an unimaginable difference. Even language itself is
part of this production. The contemporary desires are easy to
list out, as the vocabulary itself is a concordance of contemporary upset. A roof can become a "life-support system" as well
as defining an "in-between." It is residual space between the
impossible layers of rationalities. Events not part of any curric-
ulum, any continuum, any recognizable architectural project
become another space for the unfolding of a myriad other
events. The prattle is not a foregone architecture, however De-
leuzian it sounds. But we must remember that the language
is always more formidable and predictable than the architecture itself, and precisely because of this seduction should be

resisted: "The new event is produced not through collage and recollage," Tschumi has it, "but through cross-programming and transprogramming."

Perhaps we have arrived by accident to William Gibson's Drome, where "no one's talkin' human anymore." As with much contemporary thinking and discourse, the language has become easier to reach and inhabit than the architecture. The original is always a commentary of past creativity, but it is no less powerful:

The forceful images of Deleuze's thinking—the nomadic, the war machine, the rhizome—point towards the tantalizingly provocative idea of an architecture of the event. In a world that incessantly consumes images, in a constantly expanding metropolitan culture, in a universe whose buildings are no more than a few of the infinite number of figurative and informative dwellings that surround us, there nonetheless exists the architectonic event."[34]

And this event will script the fashion show and the interdisciplinarity of architecture as quickly as the thinness of application will again claim architecture to be all about space. Repetition will be inane unless informed; the ennui of the wallpaper will ensure hierarchy even out there on the mille plateaux as it is ruthlessly reassembled for a swimming pool library or a Hotel Architecture.[35]

The warning works both ways. The ease with which we assume membership with ideas and theories through vocabulary, dazzling images, and language games does not necessarily eradicate future thrill in the architectural program. Fortunately, the usefulness of redundancy ensures that the architecture must ride all claims to its own problematization of meaning and convention. Architecture problematizing architectural meaning itself still takes forms that must fight their own signification. Radical montage—if we call it that—could move beyond the parallels of film with architecture. It could move beyond the sequential movement of the observer, a rather tame promenade that lifts the catwalk into the metropolis. This type of *ciné-praxis* could attempt nomadic architectures beyond a conventional cinematic movement and montage. If we can speak seriously of unrest, and the serious poetics film brings to this project, we should be allowed to consider an architecture in continuous movement. Tschumi allows us to come full circle. This could lead to an architecture of similar weight as the fireworks, lasting only for the time it takes to note its hint of architectural form. Then—puff—like a magic dragon, architecture without any permanent meaning. The best, the most radical, in this thinking-through is doubtlessly yet to come and may not completely abandon ethical concerns.

As we stop traveling because we travel endlessly, we begin to have and need more confidence in our own unrest. Thrust into instability at every moment, politically, culturally, and often personally, this is recognizable in Tibetan thinking as the challenge of the *bardo*. The word *bardo* is commonly used to describe the intermediate state beneath death and rebirth, but in reality, Sogyal Rinpoche tells us, "bardos are occurring continuously throughout both life and death, and are junctures when the possibility of liberation, or enlightenment, is heightened."[9] Though it has never really been a problem for architecture to keep the conversation going, surely it is now even more urgent to recognize the stage in architecture when the bull of

incongruity meets the interval, as in Samuel Beckett's *Waiting
for Godot,* where nothing happens twice.[36] When considering
nomadic architectures, this is what an architecture of the event,
an architecture of sequencing and migrancy, a polyphonic choreography all begin to have in common with a liberating but
tamed chaos. We speak here of an invisible architecture revealing hidden complexities, that sort of boundless-depth architecture beyond even the impossible. This is not the architecture
of the promenade nor cubist simultaneity. Specific to cinema,
this is architecture as a pause, as a "gap" itself.

Everyone might have their favorites of those practicing architecture today who might be aiming in this direction, but
it seems that Koolhaas and Tschumi have been in the vanguard
of such ideas. From different departures they are taking architecture into event-ual invisibility. And one thing is certain—
the architectural thrill and surprise are still nascent. We haven't
seen what is so clearly waiting to emerge: "for the great thing
about the bull is that it does not have the reciprocity all on one
side—or the folly all on one side."[37] If this means destabilized
buildings with no precondition of stability, if this means
phrases like architecture problematizing meaning, if this means
architecture rejecting all a priori signification, if this means
buildings unfolding from within where a transparency codes
all spaces and event, then more and more people on the other
side of the millennium will not understand why all architects
cannot see themselves capturing a continuous series of changing perceptions.

The public naturally will not come along so quickly. And
why should they after last century's promise of architectural
reality? No amount of sophisticated cyber play or ideas of the

architect as Squatter, Hacker, or Zapper will gain further credibility in a public so confused and betrayed by architectural promise or arrogance. Instead, architecture will build into its program a way to help its public imagine the comfort as much as the horror of future nostalgia.

Undressed Architectures

We have mentioned the possibility of an architecture hijacked by film as another pornography of flight. "He is juxtaposing scenes that are discontinuous," Mamet says, "and that juxtaposition gives us a third idea." Users, like the cinemagoers, may not want to read architecture as they would a sign. As in film, where the main concern is to watch a movie, they want to inhabit a building and forego a lecture in public access, phenomenology, and symbolic import. A third vision resulting from the interrelations between film and architecture might be seen as another "discontinuous" poetics entirely. This we might call undressed architectures. There are various other uncomfortable terms for this, understood and misunderstood: *cinetectonics,* for example, might be one. However, the ambiguity of the jargon should not confuse us. Architecture can be housed by cinema, by dwelling, by language and—by Heidegger.

The traffic in Heidegger and Deleuze, the traffic in Gaston Bachelard and Benjamin, the traffic in Derrida and Jean Baudrillard, the images of their thought and the thought of their images, have allowed architecture to rediscover the "unnecessary" usefulness of, among others, film ideas, philosophy, and theory. They contribute to our ever-changing, ever-correcting,

descriptive vocabulary in architecture. Climb up the ladder
and then push it away. As a crutch to metaphysical scheming
and architectonic alibi, as a holding space warding off any further utopias, it is always difficult to see where one critical term
leaves off and another takes over. Phraseology becomes authentic and then self-destructs. Surely this is how it should be if
we are to release ourselves from the very language we think
has straitjacketed architecture. For what do we do with such
a line from Baudrillard: "The screen of history fluctuates at
the same irregular rhythm as natural phenomena"?[38]

The descriptive vocabulary available from film theory and
practice is probably familiar to many. Read any recent journal
and there will be more than a sprinkling of these terms—
spatial narrative, spatial patterning, structure, suture, the spectacle in motion, the unfolding of space in time, assemblage,
thematic/disruptive montage, depth compositions, folds, mechanical succession of instants, dialectical disorder of poses,
continuity/discontinuity, still images, utopian and chiliastic
thought, phenomenological space, the poetics of fades, cuts
versus dissolves, cineastic space, (a)temporality, and so on. We
have options, though. Exploring these concepts and allowing
them to translate themselves into possible and impossible architectures looks exciting, if the authenticity of the jargon is
not allowed to settle too hastily. Use them, navigate them,
confuse them. Understanding the differences between "scene"
and "screen" could produce differing improbable, even per-
formative, architectures. Released from inhabiting notions of
permanence, the Tibetan bardo, negotiating sense and non-
sense simultaneously, could take architecture beyond thin poetic allusions to a cinematic perception. In this way Herzog and

de Meuron's claim to get rid of the "idea" and achieve "direct communication" within their architecture needs taking seriously. This is a project beyond an applied semantic repertoire, beyond semiotics and architectural symbolism. And if we then find ourselves beyond the screen walls, however interactive—the architect as Hacker—then we push on. Architectural nullity has never held such a void as seductive, as infinite, as now.

As Paul Virilio suggested in *The Lost Dimension* via yet one more return to one of the most used and abused phrases of this century, the degree zero:

These performances and electronic video-performances are matched only by the architectural nullity of all buildings. This is the nullity we see in the arrangement of Silicon Valley, the electronic suburb of an agglomeration without agglomeration. We have arrived, in the era of telematic non-separability, at the zero degree of architecture.[39]

Such nullity, such zero degree of architecture, is no longer the cul-de-sac it implies. Instead it is rebirth time, opening as it does locked images. In effect, if we deflect the architectural jargon on the subject this might be what some well-known architects have already probed. Tschumi introduced us to the analogy of film and architecture, where events with allegorical content disturbed the neutral logic of photography. Those coming after are left to ask the obvious: Can any final meaning in architecture be cumulative and restless at the same time? No synthesis between form and function, no homogeneous signifier!

Tschumi and Koolhaas have rescripted architecture with more than filmic props. As serious unrest, and if we accept the language gaming, such attempts can dislodge architecture's traditional scenic and epistemic comfort. But this is a metaphysical trick beyond the realm of architecture itself. It is a rare flight that can only find its parachuted results much later. Architecture for the squatted mind that this implies is far from easy to grasp, but this will not make it less impossible. In "undressed" terms, this is an architecture of no frozen rituals, where the heterogeneity of movement happens whether we like it or not, or where even a contract with the prattle—the other unrelated architectural bull—needs to be taken seriously.

Perhaps transcending such literary follies was what Peter Eisenman had in mind when an automatic "narrativism" took over from a syntactic theatricality. Using C. S. Peirce's terminology, for Eisenman the symbolic—a co-opted icon—passed over to the indexical. Architecture loans from, and then interferes with, film itself (as it did with literary theory and philosophy) to become a series of temporal perceptions. When Eisenman takes it beyond an accessible methodics in architecture, we might get more than formulations of a philosophical sense. Certainly Eisenman "minds the gap" as we approach the contemporary modes of a building that must finally remain undressed, but which also at the same time undresses the metaphysical non-sense claimed for such maneuvers. The work of Libeskind comes more to mind when considering such radical resiting and undressing of architecture's upsettable meanings. Libeskind suggests buildings where whole environments become mnemonic in the past and future tense. This might become more radical traveling. An architecture occupying within a mental space past, present, and future events rather than coloristic or spatial experiences. Libeskind attempts what Witold Gombrowicz did with the Polish language. It is by no means sure that it is redundant, or even slight, to the architectural future.[40]

What might, then, we have in mind for an undressed architecture caught between Deleuze's movement-image and a liquid architecture, including sotware projections, communing deep structures and formative myths only with ourselves? Where there is no ultimate reason or concern to establish facts true to the human mind, we are left with but a wavering complexity—filmic interference as an architectural alibi, celebrated as another shifting, damning refuge. The more radical agenda this suggests remains open but was always scripted by John Hejduk in his drawn and (un)imagined architectures. Hejduk relentlessly explored new attempts to articulate this, as yet, ambiguous "liquid-upset" myth-unforming architecture. Hejduk's lesson remains relevant. He began the project of formulating architecture as a philosophical container for a contemporary unrest while at the same time acknowledging the very folly of this witness.

Architecture, damn it! *C'est la folie!* There is only one way, according to John Hejduk and Pooh Bear, to turn a minus into a plus. And it's not over your shoulder. However, we are likely to spend much of the first half of the twenty-first century exploring the errors of the last through Hejduk's layered architectures—for *the bull, in its self-cancelation, may not be poison and antidote, but it is fecundating and abortifacient.*[41] Treating architecture as another embodiment in language of life in death and death in life, Hejduk is the architect who fits best the architectural bull and bardo.[42]

Private Architectures

We arrive now at what is our fourth vision, our fourth interaction and thinking-through, in the oscillating hijack between
film and architecture. This is the realm of private architectures,
a realm of performed and performing interruptions. Here film
becomes an aid toward serious, inner, hallucinating instability.
The liquid trauma of an earthquake or the flight simulation
machine at a funfair are mere child's play in such private architectural imagination, response, and vision. Displacement and
disjunction have already become a continuous form of interpreting movement if we have followed the first three visions.
We are left here with a proposed world on permanent skew,
pulled back to itself but always resisting nostalgia or necro-
philia. When the collective has become so private, the private
begins to seek newer isolation. When Frank Gehry's son tells
him he thinks he might be living as part of the "Last Generation," it is this we have in mind. The future is out there, but
no one is home. Universal Studios in Los Angeles is only one
version of the collective ciné-city. This is not what we have in
mind. As a collective experience, the private realm offers more
disruptive futures. Here, our private worlds will continue to
meet and collide with the technology of the imaginary. The
failure to be fixed is going to continue disfiguring our own
worlds. Privileged direction may be private, nature might invest
culture with its own unrest. Cities might abdicate their privileges. We are as unclear about it as architecture is at present.
But, of course, and here is the catch, it is essential to be unclear
about such a shift if we are to follow the logic of the very discipline of unrest and movement we have begun exploring.

Over the last decade or so there have been any number of writings about this imaginary world. Take, for example, Luigi Lentini, in his essay "Private Worlds and the Technology of the Imaginary." Lentini talked some time ago of a "total soliloquy, in which a subject talks to his or her own electronic image . . ." This is already more than possible. And as disruptive as this has become, it is not necessarily disturbing to the extent some of us might fear. Future environments created by data gloves and personal virtual reality kits are the glossy Sony Corporation end of something quite extraordinary. They vanish as quickly as they create the next stage. Events and environments produced might be so sensitive that users feel the texture and enter the space of an, at present, unimaginable architecture. It is also possible that no writing will keep up with the ongoing experiments and no experience will be shared. Even critical journalism itself could trail and not dictate such imaginary architecture, so far from any generic architecture of the surface this might become. Exploring electronics and manipulating software rather than exalting engineering are phrases that will not only haunt Venturi but all of us well into this new millennium.

An unimaginable architecture, however, does not mean that its accommodation to iconography will remain so tame or be realized hastily on this, the other side of the year 2000. Neither does this mean an unimaginable future brought about by the Disney "imagineers." In the early part of the twentieth century, these "imagineers" were not working for Disney or the Dream Factory, they were people like the Portuguese poet Fernando Pessoa. As Bernardo Soares, Pessoa anticipated such an unimaginable environmental space, scripting a private menu that

architecture has no option but to respond to. This was an interrupted architecture of dream with a serious logic of unrest:

Sometimes I dream how agreeable it would be, in my dreams, to
create a second interrupted life for myself, where I would spend entire
days with imaginary fellow travellers, totally fabricated people, and I
would live, suffer, and take pleasure from that fictive life. In that
world, sadness would happen, huge joys would fall on me. And nothing of me would be real. But everything there would possess a superb
serious logic, all would dance to the rhythm of voluptuous falsehood,
all would take place in a city made up out of my very soul, which
would go and vanish away on the platform beside a peaceful train,
far off inside me, very far off . . . And all would be clear, inevitable,
the outside life, except the aesthetics of the Death of the Sun.[43]

Even in the beginning of a new millennium, wouldn't we
be foolish to think this important only to those with a passing
interest in modern thought and the last century? If we thought
we understood the architecture of Beckett, Vladimir Nabokov,
Luigi Pirandello, Pessoa, and Thomas Pynchon, Don De Lillo
and V. S. Naipaul, we might be in for a surprise. Are we so
warned? Perhaps we shouldn't even think of feeling or dream-
ing such architecture! To "download some essence of timeless
hyperspace," Rushkoff has it, into a form we can all understand, in linear reality, might be our own hopeful unprejudiced
project called privacy. We are not clearly all would-be ushers
of the Final Paradigm, nor would many of us know what to
do when Surfers Unite becomes the architectural slogan.
Members of rave culture may have been phase-locked by
changing their circadian rhythms, which leaves architects pre-

cisely nowhere, if not at the fractal end of the surface. Ethically, this is all uncharted ground. In the privacy project, architecture shares with the "Go Zen!" raver the object of dancing—no purpose, no agenda. Information passed around in the privacy project will always be less important than the way it is passed around. Hyperradicality will resemble the architecture of the computer-with-will. Structure will recede, texture will reappear, the pleasure of architecture, private bliss, and surface desire will be the logical and desolate responses to the fractal universe. An empty territory?[44] Architecture for nothing! And in the symposiums, when people wonder what everyone will talk about, they will miss the point that it is actually happening in front of them. Too many of us probably leapfrog the present we try so desperately to hold on to. No separation between dance and movement, song and meaning, deck and existence. This *is* the meaning.

Does this bring us full circle via our four visions and interferences? Should architecture, as we continue to think we know it, as the public individual and collective believes it, be abandoned? Is telematics and telepresence about to dissolve our own relationships in a space we cannot grasp, in a space we can no longer feel lonely within, in a gender we now have no right to inhabit? Perhaps architecture already has been abandoned, way way beyond any electronic shed and we are now chasing its own discourse in order to establish and reconfirm its own disaster. Of course it isn't necessarily too late. Like a stage in one of the Tibetan bardos, imagination also has a way of pulling back, which death will not obey. Around the corner of the next millennium, the collective will surely even out. The reality of a latent world—always this deferred world, a world shared with cinema too—will be personal, virtual, and fragmented. It might be a never-ending variation on Adorno's liberated and fragmented mankind, where dream, space, and technology offer personal menus for an architecture as yet untheorized. The firework is our joy, the sparkler in our hand only the managable, controllable event of an otherwise spiraling world full of architectures unimagined—even redundant—but performing in front of us. Architecture beyond architecture as we know it?

Is the power glove leading to a fantasy architecture accelerated by media shows and journalism? In Gore Vidal's novel *Duluth,* there is a CIA mole named Roland Barthes who goes wrong in a word-processing program. However, we are much further than this. Vonnegut, Venturi, and Vidal are taken over by Virilio. Living, housing, and dwelling may be uncinematic only because present-day housing is in essence cinematic. If there are ways that film theory and thinking have hijacked and leapfrogged our collective psyches through the televisual satelliting world network, a scenographic architecture might be the mere edge. Medial or irremedial facades suggest quite promising as well as frightening architectures to come. These imaginary architectures beyond us become a reality faster than we could possibly imagine.

Be an architect, more than a rumor! Architecture is, as ever, already controlled by forces and trends beyond its own domain. Take the Circle Line and "mind the gap," but the train never stops. The architect as a Deconstructor in the House of Follies was acceptable—we could keep up with that. We could even continue living as all the crash-angle architecture became fraudulent sculpture. But the architect as a Hacker in the Digital House, the architect as Squatter? The enigma of the Electronic Arrival, as the commentators call it, is the fourth world of architectural promise. It has become the essence of the housed being—personal, interactive: therefore I am, cinema. Beyond the rumors of thinking with movement or thinking as movement, we inhabit thinking under shock, a radically new politics of everyday space and interrogation. This is a pornography, if you like, of unseen flight, where cyberspace comes true.

Even our advice for architecture's visions can come from film stars rather than the critics, from the East, not the West. As Sam Shepard once said in an interview, "There is this thing about L.A. It is immune. No matter what you say about it, it is going to keep on being degenerate and depraved." Here is the final clue in this intervention within architecture. Film will undo more than its own thinking, and redundancy will never be so redundant. And for the embarrassment and the immunity of future architecture, we could do no better than alter Sam Shepard's own lines about Los Angeles: Architecture here has become the architecture it's pretending to be!

2 **no text where none intended** *interrogating photography and architecture*

Architecture talks a good game; film helps it along. Photography has been doing it for years. In much contemporary architectural debate, talking a good game often leaves us with a special kind of ecstasy, an ecstasy of no further communication. We sigh and again think of William's Gibson's line, "But nobody's talkin' human, see!" However, such bullish absurd ecstasy is approachable. As Samuel Johnson said of his visit to Wales, "I am glad that I have seen it, though I have seen nothing, because I now know there is nothing to be seen."[1]

The possibility of no further communication leaves film and other disciplines the options to work out what we thought was impicit all along in architecture—communication itself. It is hard to tell at which stage architecture ceased taking communication for granted. Suspicion that communication is not so straight-arrow red-bull certain is a good sign. We can even be pleased about no further communication, a stage, if you like, where we must stop taking *anything* for granted in architecture. Is it not this that Jacques Herzog has in mind when he uses the term *direct communication?* No text where none intended?

Photography, too, has played its role in lending support to a communication act much debated, much suspected. And photography has certainly led architect, thinker, and layman alike to continue reading architecture primarily from aspects of a visual seduction, expecting those optical truths László Moholy-Nagy dreamed of in the 1920s: "Thus in the photographic camera we have the most reliable aid to a beginning of objective vision. Everyone will be compelled to see that which is optically true, is explicable in its own terms, is objective, before he can arrive at any possible subjective positions."[2]

It has always been problematic to tell where the camera leaves off and architecture begins. The lamentations we meet about photography's cruel, manipulative ambiguity do not quite erase the compelling necessity to imagine the "optically true." It was doubtless as difficult for those in 1925 to imagine the insatiability of images that we live in today, as it must now seem equally difficult today to imagine the passion with which that objective vision was sought then. It was this very insatiability of the photograph that compelled Susan Sontag (in 1977), John Berger (in 1980), and Roland Barthes (in 1981) to write passionate pleas for controlling (or pretending to control) the wilfulness of subjective positions forced on us by photography.

John Berger, always a fine analyst of "looking," produced a collection of pieces in *About Looking*.[3] Despite a Marxist critique of late capitalism, the photograph as the eye of the capitalist God, Berger wrote an essay called "The Uses of Photography," some observations on Susan Sontag's book *On Photography*. Interspersing his own comments within Sontag's, Berger identified the loss of meaning in the photographic event as one of a serious relationship to memory: "What photographs do out there in space was previously done with reflection." Neither preserving meaning, narrating, or arresting meaning, Berger suggested the obvious—a plural, radial approach to bring relevance back to the photograph. The hopelessness in this approach implied a diversity, an increased way to occupy the photograph so that it could be seen in terms that are "simultaneously personal, political, economic, dramatic, everyday, and historic."

From the strong redemptive strategies of Berger and Sontag, it was left to Roland Barthes to remind us that our scan-
ning methods, our own ways of reading photographs, tend to
confirm those appearances that suit our own measure. Almost
twenty years ago, the cover blurb on Barthes's book *Camera
Lucida* interprets it as "coolly personal . . . yet astonishingly
inclusive." It considers Barthes to have offered a "kind of dismayed justice to the sane role of photography among us."[4]
Actually, Barthes's approach was more interesting for the ways
he struggled with the doxa (public opinion) so much invoked
in his own discourse than it was for the inclusive generalizations and reflections on photography itself. Barthes celebrated
this semantic freedom of photography for a personal desire,
spectacularly and idiosyncratically reading fictions into the
photograph that came from other worlds. Barthes used the
photograph like a cemetery, an intermediate zone, a gap in
which he knew he could locate a liminal ecstasy. Walking
within it one always passes to the other world.

Barthes's own desire, however, should not deflect us too
rapidly and cause instant dismay. And were we to think that
this dismay in photography threatens the very act we would
be mistaken. It is mysterious to posit Barthes as that docile
cultural subject trying to arrest private meaning in public photographs, while the number of books and monographs emerging on photography over the last decade has been staggeringly
enormous and looks unlikely to decrease.[5] We are thus surely
forced to redefine disaffection.

Despite last century's profound manipulative propaganda of
radicalism, photography's failure can be seen as part of the

gradual deradicalization of the twentieth century. Like the demedicalization of society and death, analyzed by Ivan Illich in the 1970s, the critical alarm about photography has been mostly confined to the intelligentsia. Only occasionally have the astonishing facts, already established in 1855, that photographs could lie, negatives could be touched up, reality blurred, had any contact to the wider public. Although photography generates works that can be called art, as Sontag says, "[P]hotography is not, to begin with, an art form at all. Like language, it is a medium in which works of art (among other things) are made. . . . it requires subjectivity, it can lie, it gives gives aesthetic pleasure."[6] Egged on by this seduction, the public in all likelihood, also encouraged by "advanced photo systems" and other technological bluff, seem to prefer the hallucinated reality of photography to any sense of genuine disaffection. Which means, given the closed delinquency of this outrage, that the disaffection of photography's craft and the manipulation of its inevitable surrealism remain confined to a smaller and smaller public. Any amount of intensity in video art installations indicates that artists and students are redefining the insatiability of images and photography's more conventional roles. Disaffection is simply no longer an issue, as it is subsumed within plurality, fragmentation, and resistance to optical seduction. And if this delinquency is likely to be overtaken by the interactive vibrancy and radicality of video art, we must inquire into the startling consequence that architecture looks likely to remain loyal to photography's naive optical seduction longer than this disaffection ever imagined.

A further consequence of such loyalty we may find difficult to acknowledge: all architecture aspires to the condition of photography and not vice versa. The photograph might have been to Berger (and Barthes) a memento from a life being lived. However, shifting this deathly sentence to architecture, it suggests that photography always lifts the building out of time, out of breath. Lifted out of its function, without this radiality, photographing architecture will inevitably invite disinterest and disaffection. Unless privately experienced, architectural photography would then be deranged. Addressing this by perhaps shooting architecture from the hip hardly exists in the controlled outlets for the stylized architectural photograph.

Photography has never been truly represented by the coffee-table book only. This also applies massively to architecture. Neither were the secrets of soul and message in photography exhausted by the texts rip-cording out from the structuralist inquiries of the 1950s. Ideologically, a photograph may be mute until something external points up an emphasis, but it was Walter Benjamin who identified the ever-present slide and attempt to arrest photography, "to fix fleeting reflections." Hostility about photographs not being allowed to communicate, or artists not stamping their intentions on their work, indicate a failure to understand communication itself. Here film echoes photography, for there is no real way to distinguish between suitable and unsuitable viewers. The consequences of this to architecture have been devastating. The lack of any clear meaning in the photograph has not only been given mystical status; it has given a privilege to architecture that it cannot always support: "If modern eyes are lit up like shop windows, "Beatriz Colomina puts it, "so too are the windows of modern architecture."[7]

Photography has never had an authentic jargon. The very ambiguity of its performance forbids this, ensuring that its authenticity proceeds symbiotically, countering tradition with revolution. Photography's authenticity comes along with crutches, with the opportunist photographer often lost somewhere in between tradition and revolution. This problematic status of photography is elegantly shown by Colomina in her research and interpretation of Adolf Loos:

It is perhaps for that reason that Loos insists, in a passage almost mysteriously omitted from the English translation of his famous text, *Architektur,* that the interior is that which cannot be photographed: *the inhabitants of my interiors do not recognise their own house in photographs.* The interior is disguised by the photograph in the same way that, for Saussure, the photograph that is writing veils speech. . . . If, for Saussure, writing is the photography of speech, and for Loos the interior is that which cannot be photographed, for Sitte "modern" urban space is the photograph of the "place." The "outside" is a photographic image. The mask is first and foremost a picture.[8]

To extend this, the mask can also be seen in the intermediate of photography as a moving-picture always fleetingly held back by architecture. Benjamin was perhaps the first to observe how much easier architecture could be grasped in photographs than in reality. From Saussure through to Barthes, it is possible that the ideal of an architecture communicated unambiguously through various codes and practices and the mystic privilege given to photography have done away with any intermediate realm. The ecstasy has gone even further astray, and we should heed the warning given by Solà-Morales, "Today's work of architecture is no longer the result of a magical action."[9] Look, for example, at how Hélène Binet wedges nonmeaning and the architectural bull into photographs of the work of Libeskind, Zaha Hadid, Peter Zumthor, and Hejduk. "She," Binet says of Hadid, "urged me not to ignore the foundations and messiness of the buildings in favour of harmonious, completed building images."[10]

A realm where individuals must find their own appropriate relationship to architecture, zones of opacity, zones of incommunicability, zones where meaning fluctuates, no longer underwrites a tragic aspect to architecture. It no longer makes sense to continue denying as helpful to architecture its continuing fluctuations in meaning and intention, its loss in magic. Clearly, an architecture no longer interested in stabilizing meaning can of course—momentarily—be arrested by photography. Yet such a state encouraged by the very ambiguity of the photographic mission must be able to interfere with conventions. The photograph may have become architecture's pretext, but can it ever compensate for idle language left lying around the corridors of broken dreams?

Despite the ever-present manipulation, photography begs the following question: Can and does it lead to changes in architectural language itself? Colomina asks:

What can architecture for magazines be when the magazine uses photography as its medium? Does the photographic transformation of architecture do no more than present it in a new vision, or is there a deeper transformation, a sort of conceptual agreement between the space this architecture comprehends and the one implicit in photography?[11]

In the 1980s, an urge to narrativize photography before you could do it yourself saw its appearance in art shows and museums throughout the world. Among others writing and theorizing on photography, Victor Burgin put photography into the thinking league. The conceptual performance of a photograph was measured and celebrated. Photography attested to its own arrested development at a time when the full "coding" catastrophe of semiosis infiltrated just about every sign system. Philosophy was read from the absence of the photographic surface. Though Barthes, Sontag, and Burgin shared with many the obvious suspicion of photography, none made the mistake of thinking they were photographically correct. None made the mistake of thinking that now, right now, communication is more possible than it was. And none made the mistake of thinking only this photograph communicates, whereas the other is mute. All recognized, with varying urgency and regret, that the democracy in photography was its own flight of meaning.

Contemporary evidence and a general disillusion with straight-arrow communication supports a longer, wiser review of photography's semantic traps and the architectural seduction within photography. Nothing can arrest the democracy within photography itself, and nothing can suggest where meaning leaves off and irresponsibility takes over. The democracy of the photograph must include accident, titillation, predictability, stupidity, and frivolity as much as fragility, detachment, disfiguration, and responsibility. In this way, photography is redundant to architecture but essential in our "detective" scheme of things.

More importantly, photography started contesting itself around the time that much architectural photography opted for a form of harmonious scenography. An obvious paradox resulted. If, as was claimed, the photograph ultimately serves only the private use of the public instrument, if it was so dispersed *and* disordered as to resist only the meanings we apply to its surface or messages that we like to skim off for our own sentiment and ecstasy, then its role in architecture would appear inevitably doomed. Surely, photography would then have no option but to predispose a way of seeing architecture that in turn becomes a way of ignoring those parts—for professionals—that do not photograph. Strictly speaking, there should be no optical truth in any fragmented, cropped, framed, and touched-up version of any building; there should only be traces of a moment that went before and never came again. But, and here we are involved in the very act of deradicalism, this image insatiability has not really extended to the production of architecture.

True, technology, even Canon's *Advanced Photo System,* allows the illusion of control, the ability to improve on what one can achieve. The "advanced photo system" actually offers the formats the architectural photographer has had available for years by using special equipment and varying lenses. The result of this is not only the demystification of the panorama and less badly focussed choir practices, birthday parties, or harbor scenes. The result may also be an ennui faster than we can predict, even though, between the lines, any advanced system offers "advanced" results. In other words, we get better, sharper images and color, better grains and lighting performance, which in turn leads to the illusory advance of photography—increased aesthetic pleasure and seduction.

It will not be long before all images can be corrected (improved?) to conform to the imagined image not of what you decide to take, but what the programmer decides should be the proper image setting within the camera. Whether building, choir practice, or wedding, format and lighting will be as adjustable, and thus as cinematic, as required. The private photogaph ("snap," if you prefer) will become what the architectural photograph already is—polished, manipulatable, sentimental, and dead. Both will converge and become steadily, even predictably, conventional. All identical with the wall, as Miroslav Holub says:

Paintings on walls.
Saroyan in a frame, Beckett in a frame.
Breughel in a frame.
Mummy, when she was twenty, framed,
me, when I was six, framed.

All
dead
for
ages.

And identical with the wall.[12]

The photograph is hallucinatory, it is mnemonic, it talks not to those who have either been there or done it, but those who have seen it. If it is uncertain whether photography has enlarged our vision of what architecture could be or served prettier lies, more certain is that the conventionalism of the architectural photograph confirms the sentimental within architecture. This conventionalism has also helped along the hopeless promise of those optically true versions of a modernism fixed somewhere in the 1920s. Stretching a point, the ethics of *seeing* architecture, not *experiencing* architecture, has in no small way been responsible for the dreadfully confused and confusing press that the new century is likely to serve on twentieth century architecture. Susan Sontag punishingly compells photography to little more than a surrealist whim but suggests the necessity of an "ecology of images." Perhaps this prompted John Berger's radiality, a photograph seen in terms simultaneously personal and political, everyday and historic. We think we know what he means until we attend to our own measure and realize issues are cancelled out by their very whim. Barthes considered all this, including whim, a necessary disorder in photography that we must attend to personally in order to accept that photography can be mad or sane, wild or well behaved.

Without any special intentionality, without the cultural baggage we bring along to the photograph, there is, of course, no text where none intended. Which is why, with a photograph, we are always literally and metaphorically in the middle, and why we are more likely to attend to our own (structural— momentary?) way of arresting meaning than someone else's.

It has always been considered unquestionable to see the photograph as fixed, as motionless. Just as we are attracted to the close-to-meaninglessness in photographs, so was Barthes: "When we define the photograph as a motionless image, this does not mean only that the figures it represents do not move; it means that they do not emerge, do not leave. They are anes-

theticized and fastened down, like butterflies." Yet hasn't
Barthes himself been overtaken by the insatiability of the image? Looking at a photograph is like entering an ongoing conversation. No longer pinned down like a butterfly, it is an
oscillation as much as an interference. Starting in the middle
means some way past the beginning, some way before the end.
Usually when we attempt to "read" a photograph, we scan
and read both backward and forward, slantingly as if there is
a beginning, as if there is an end. And where no text is intended
we supply one, we invent one, we script one. Even with the
virtuous plain architectural record we do this no less.

Shut your eyes and try to recall. Little rebounds back in
photography's homogeneity. Paradoxically, in this way, photography shuts out architecture. As we clear things from our
mind by dominating them, completing them, photography
tempts us toward the visually obvious and familiar. The magical nature fades, the hallucinatory is harder to maintain as architecture and building face manipulation and control at every
stage of production.

It cannot, though, surely be acceptable for us to remain in
an accusatory mode. However debilitating this lament against
photography's mission can become professionally, we must attempt a more contemporary critique of the pact between architecture and photography, a pact that by nature of its
irreversible contract with technology means that everything
can be touched up, enhanced, or reversed, to the extent that
the dull is duller, the bright is brighter, the trivial more trivial,
and the sentiment more sentimental.

Photography may be the "reality"—the architectural experience—for most people of most buildings, yet our disappoint-

ment differs, individually, culturally. A photograph of Karnak
or the Taj Mahal probably disappoints less than a photograph
of Lloyd's of London on a dull grey London day. There is a
professional pain experienced with photography that cannot
be translated into general terms. Those—mostly architects—
who suspect the magic (a professional hazard) find that the
photograph falls short of "capturing" their vision of the building, their vision of architecture. It might be fragmental, un-
inclusive, even synecdochical. The vocabulary is personal, the
failure tacit. The very brevity of an architectural photograph
serves unrest. Imagine how many times one has heard the
phrase, "It's not photographable!" There is always that tragic
delay, the "gap" that puts a photograph further away in
shadow land than the reality within architecture itself.

We live with the irreversible knowledge that images can be
tampered with.[13] Even if they are not, the possibility indicates
constant critical vigilance, constant critical sharpness. This is
not a cynical position, it is a foreknowledge that warns us of
early seduction, of early promise. Accepted in architecture, this
is often bypassed in order to hallucinate an architectural promise gained from beyond its own production.

There are interesting, not entirely contradictory, statements
from Susan Sontag that can help us configure the hallucinatory
relations to the architectural photograph: "To take a picture
is to have an interest in things as they are, in the status quo
remaining unchanged." Many architectural photographers
would probably deny this, opting for the opportunity to intervene in this process, opting for the auteur strategy. By so doing,
does the photographer merely fondle the status quo into suggesting change? If this is illusory, as Sontag's argument contin-

ues, if photography has vastly enlarged our notion of what is aesthetically pleasing, is this "in the name of prettier lies?"[14]

How does one approach the photography of a building? The sophisticated disaffection of photography, at professional cost and narrowness, may remain unattended. Despite lamentable ambiguity, the professional architectural photographer mostly opts for the "auteur" approach and many, directly or indirectly, still occupy the Moholy-Nagy position. The lecturer has a different approach to the framed image than the architectural photographer. The approach to the photograph also differs if intended for a slide show, a detailed lecture, a photo essay, brochure, postcard, or personal memento. Depending on the status and cultural and social history of the building, lecturers approach the image differently from editors. Accepting time and agenda, do these approaches, albeit in miniature, differ from any cinematographer?

To some, the whole sequence must be viewed cinematically, linearly, as if the roving eye is caught by the still photographer, as if the video freeze offers more educational possibility. To others, the fragment or main shot will suffice. Of course, light and seasonal variations can transform the buildings, as can events taking place. We might describe the photographic capture of a building a natural progression in four stages. This is linear, though it need not be the case.

The first order, the establishing shots, usually indicate mass, totality, and an immediate, predictable (often erroneous) idea of scale. By framing and clues to scale, the size of the building is revealed or mystified. There is danger in this, as Mamet identifies: "Now, don't you go establishing things. Make the audience wonder what's going on by putting them in the same position as the protagonist."[15]

After the cautious establishing shot, the second order is usually the conventional photographic rhetoric found in journals. This is the frontal image, whether, in fact, the front or the back of a building. Usually main shots, entrances, large exteriors, (corrected or altered) wide angles, these are often tacit, culture bound, and represent the satisfactory, even average (accessible), effect of architecture. The photography itself can be and often is far from average. Here a homogeneity in architectural images remains cultural, professional, and undisturbed. In Barthes's words, they don't really touch us! These photographs conform to the profession's way of drawing, and thus seeing elevations, however much this has been challenged in recent theory.

The third order of architectural approach in photography is in the detail. Applicable to space, material, and construction, this level automatically invites further messages to be taken, even showing one detail to suggest another, more general world. Titillatory, in the small we can see or deny the whole. And if denied, then it also invites the obvious next level of photographic "capture."

The fourth order in our sketch of architectural photography would then be the invisible, often unaccounted for, detail that we could call the accident. Something might happen, might be stumbled across, that invites the photographer to take an image. It might be planned, noticed, even staged. It might be fleeting, unique, and unstaged. The very act of photography, however, then cancels out the accidental, immediately inviting the suspicion of the "orchestrated."

No photograph resulting from these four stages can actually say what it intended. Photography is subversive not when it frightens, repels, or even stigmatizes, as Barthes says, but when it is pensive, when it thinks. Insatiability has had its consequences even on this. Barthes was only partially correct. Photography is probably subversive the closer to the meaningless it takes us. Perhaps the closer we get to the blind spots of photography, the closer we get to the blind spots of architecture.

We load a film, aim it, and shoot it. But we rarely do this when shooting architecture. Professionals wait for the sun to dial a cliché; amateurs group around the picture points. Buildings may not have a morality in the way a person has, but they have a vulnerability. Image choked, the architectural photographer may attempt a self-canceling exercise, but the amateur opts for more nostalgia and familiarity than ever. Rarely do we get a comparative photography, the dull day against rain or the sunny day against the overcast. Any form of early interactive studies of buildings and architecture that the camera could have offered since 1925 have been rare. In the twentieth century, an optical truth inextricably tied with the professional production and promise of architecture ruled out other ways of photographic seeing. We got either an architectural surveillance or memorialization.

If the convention of a building's sign outweighs its surprise, what then of its photography? Do we already sense failure? If we consider the building "avant-garde," what can a photograph add to this? And what, in the way the photograph is chosen, its format, lighting, mood, and mode, invites a heavy familiarity that can then be interpreted as anachronistic? What detail or angle provides more thinking or more kenosis than others? One of the reasons for such boredom with photography may be that no one is really captivated by the lifelike unless it is a form of hyperrealism. By which methods, then, do we dislodge reality to accept another version, another vision? By staging them?

Does a photograph of a building exist within the synchronic, that collecton of photographs around right now in architectural magazines, mostly of hard-edged glass and a rhetoric of minimal transparency soon to be memetically shifted to a later identifiable trend? Or does it find its slow way into the diachronic memory and resonance of previous photographs, previous architecture? Failing this current image membership can mean the architecture lacks the hard edge, the contemporary flintiness of instability. Some images of architecture will ride the moment, some will add mystery to the moment, altering scale by accident or design. Some won't even get a chance.

Laughter at the possible anachronism of architecture that defies photographic capture betrays arrogance and dull idealism. The residues within much contemporary architecture that some may think predate the modern itself will come as something of a surprise to those uncomfortable with the space of ritual itself. It is architectural unlearning time for photography. This desire for a theater of architectural images has been encouraged by the architects themselves, certifying their own existence through the relevant polish and photogenesis of their buildings, their architecture. Clearly, publishing, commissioning bodies, and educational careerism have limited the use of photography to the acceptable market reality. This is necessarily an instant and immediate access that encourages brevity and seduction rather than reflection and narrative. Limited voyeurism, supporting the status quo, this can be seen to have done little for architecture and its reception in the last century. As Sontag says, "To take a picture is to have interest in things as they are, in the status quo remaining unchanged" even if the architecture presents itself as ever changing.[16]

Of course, high-profile buildings cannot fail to become a laboratory of invested meaning, and, naturally, disappoinment. The reason for those able to experience the building can often differ from the image expected. The role photography plays in this flattening is not always clear, but it is possible precisely because photography is often considered democratic in its access. We can all read a photograph even if we are not all able to visit the building. And yet it would be naive of us to think the photograph can be pulled back to an agreed set of readings. The unphotographability of a building or architecture (the opposite of the experience of disappointment— seeing the building rather than its image and being disappointed) involves our own construction of a world that may deny or play within photography itself. This is not the surrealist exercise (Sontag) but the exercise of blurring photography's limit (the acultural Barthes).

Over the last thirty years of the twentieth century, very little in the architectural publishing scene actually helped the nonprofessional reading of images. Mostly, the way of seeing architecture through photography remained in the private and privileged world of the architects themselves. One need only remark how often people never "people" architectural

photographs but are invariably sketched in, or now "digitalized" onto perspectives and simulated exteriors and interiors.
Yet still some remain surprised that the public cannot "skim
off" the obvious messages and levels in the buildings. Surprised, too, are some when the "proper" reading of a fragment
or accident is missed, leading to all sorts of confusion about
space and the labyrinth, about ambiguity and unrest in architecture.

Only with a private interest (as we search our own photographs for familiarity, resonance, even death?) can we begin to
sketch out an image politics of the architectural photograph.
Only with an applied intentionality can we notice how the
photograph itself can be read against architecture or offer a
reading against culture. This is all made easier by captions,
of course, which heavily dislodge the photograph's openness.
Therefore, instead of investing the photograph with more and
more meaning, searching for an ecology of the image, it would
surely be more profitable to disarm the image, to seek ways of
resisting and riding the confused messages that will always be
on offer.

Photography not only doesn't touch us, sometimes it doesn't
even get near to architecture's evidence. Much contemporary
architecture shares a triumph in that no photography captures
it. Perhaps there exists such architecture that need not the photograph, nor could the photograph begin to do justice to the
poetics and experience available within the architecture. Acknowledging this, and in respect to such impossibility, could
we not see many architects designing quite different works
sharing the same fortune? In architectonic terms, those archi-

tects sharing such bull-critical language, serial architecture, and interpenetration present a problem to photography.

The overiding modernist attempt at an architecture of discontinuity within an aesthetic of continuity is and still remains (to use other words) a "flow." An architecture in movement and about movement will always present photographic difficulty. In the history of architecture, such work—a difficulty both to eye and feet, a difficulty tactile and physical—has often been repressed because it remains residual *and* enigmatic to conventional documentation. Yet photographing architecture is also something else. It obviously poses different problems with different buildings in different cultures. It becomes a currency in a picture-search world, in a world that increasingly turns the pages without reading the text.

There is a theater of world architectural images, just as there is a theater of world architectural drawings. Recent immense advances in the Internet, computer-aided design, and modeling, plus satellite communications, will further catalog and carnivalize this theater of world images to which we all belong without always being aware of it. We all continue in some way by reading, looking, and consuming, by taking photographs, slides, shooting videos and films, by writing, stuttering, and talking. It is irksome to some that we cannot avoid this memetic activity, just as architects cannot avoid the theater of images they design within. And most of us are involved in the conventional architectural photography even if only with a disposable camera without brains!

I suggested that photography may have predisposed an architectural way of seeing that has itself become a poetics of departure for architecture. A crucial point needs to be taken onboard here. Is the academic agreement that there is an exhaustion, that the photograph fails in relation to architecture, so entrenched? Probably not. It is not at all certain that this "failure" is shared by all professionals. It is also not a failure shared by those in professional control of architectural projects and production (politicians, planners, programmers, publishers, or decision makers from all the social divisions involved in architecture). The prettier lies—the seduction—the essential narrrowing of architecture to an image may be part of its eternal hopeless (hapless) political promise.

Despite the loyalty toward optical truths, how many among us still want photography to defeat architecture's sentiment, to defeat the seduction brought so easily to it? How many of us still want to bid ourselves—however irresponsible—to go further than the titillated, the predictable, the altered and accidental document of photography's fragment of a building's idleness? With no purity of seeing, no optical truths, disarming the image then demands either more carnival or more retrieval. An architectural pact with blindness or kenosis!

Perhaps this only points out once again the obvious: "no critique except among those already capable of criticism."[17] Thus no disaffection except among those already open to the dismay photography offers. Hence we reach photography's double bind on architecture: "Oh Lord, I dismay. Help my undismay." And dismayed, we will continue to use photography. Despite, or because of, the exhaustion and lamentations, the appeal to make real, photography's pact with architecture may need to go on long being ignored in architecture. It is likely, too, that architecture will remain loyal to the seduction of an optical truth. It will go on believing in architecture represented by images that speak for a promise never achieved. To go further, to go beyond dismay, might be recommended, though to do so means an unpredictable radical disarming of the photograph—an act that takes the photographer out of photography. No promise where none intended or even possible?

An irresponsible conclusion may be an arranged, staged one. In this new century everything once more will be open, no text because none no longer entered in the space where there should be one. Which is why we are not quite rid of Barthes yet: "No action or thought without thought, no aim without a target?"[18] This might be the scandalous movement favored by a critic, but it might also be the essential redundancy that produces the rarest quality, a liberating potential within a photograph—architecture's blind spot.

Taking turns with Buddha, we look into our own emptiness and retain a promise from that which is always outside us, like architecture. In Jorge Semprun's book *Literature or Life,* photography's pact with architecture is nowhere better stated, albeit obliquely. He has been asked, why do you hate me today? His reply:

I don't answer; I look at the scenery. I'm not thinking of the scenery, of course. I'm thinking about something else entirely. There's nothing to think about this scenery, I might add. It's quite lovely, and all you have to do is look at it, rejoicing in its loveliness, as you contemplate it. Unmistakable beauty inspires not thought but happiness: a kind of rapture, that's all. I'm sitting enraptured with this landscape in

Ascona spread out before me in December sunshine and I'm thinking of something else completely different."[19]

To those fortunately theoretically uninformed, to those involved in the control of reality in architectural production, this critique must seem a redundant cry. To assert such a lamentable position for architecture and photography may bear very little relation to their own reality. Traditional architectural photography, after all, involves much idling, much waiting. We might term this, after William Gibson, sundial photography: "The building becomes a kind of sundial, while you wait for a shadow to crawl away from a detail you want, or for the mass and balance of the structure to reveal itself in a certain way."[20] Yet is it only to professionals that such conventional photography appears of little thrill? Today either there is not time to wait for the sun to reveal a detail wanted, or those details are no longer required. Instead of waiting for photography to serve an architecture they think is necessary, many today feel they have already lived through a storyboard for a film about waiting and architecture. Many are in echo and on the return journey where architecture has become the event that has already happened. No longer the container, the shelter, it has become the all too brief fireworks display. What right, then, does this give us to serve sentence on photography's pact with architecture?

Where the photograph scores in architecture might be where it appeals best to the professional eye. Never more than circling in on itself, some quite stunning photography keeps us thinking we want to visit buildings we might never see. Many must have experienced the feeling of arriving at a building, well-known or not, and being disappointed. Either the building in question does not perform to the image built up or "read" from the photograph, or the building adds no more to the experience that the photograph gave. Sadly, we get so many of the latter that a neutrality results, a neutrality that has continued to feed the architectural magazine and journal over the last twenty years. It has seen an endless stream of instant twilight editions of architectural monographs claiming more for an architecture that so often wants to claim less.

In an essay called "The New Architecture," Ada Louise Huxtable describes this twilight exercise: "Nothing is more seductively appealing than being terminally iconoclastic—a lot of mileage can be gotten out of insisting that there should be no architecture at all."[21] A closer look at her acute assessments of the architects Alvaro Siza, Frank Gehry, and Christian de Portzamparc illustrate the photograph's legacy to language and architectural claim. The language invites us into the work as much as it invites us into the photograph. Just as Huxtable sees this trio absorbing what serves their needs in contemporary thinking and then going their own way, she understandably imagines architecture pictured in this way. It is not a coincidence that Huxtable actually remarks on the photography of architecture, for without the evidence of architecture she knows there is little to distinguish this work from work by other lesser-respected, even unknown architects. In the architectural theater of images little subtlety is possible. Rescue is necessary.

"These buildings must be visited personally," Huxtable writes. "Photographs are more than usually misleading; what one sees in pictures are the strange shapes and stylistic mannerisms that merely hint at the strategies beneath." Ditto for much contemporary and marginalized architecture. Gehry's "unrepentent modernism," Portzamparc's "lively retro-wit," and Siza's "elemental purity" are all claims betrayed by the photograph. Huxtable's language reinforces the point. The suitable or unsuitabie viewer will make what sense they want from an image of the work and go their own way, informed or otherwise of the strategies beneath. Huxtable's dilemma of the photographed image is partnered by the so-called orchestrated gem of a building. Photography has aided their curious, often unchallengable position in architectural publishing. Buildings are still being built in some countries with the expectation of the grand publication, the grand photographic job. Long ago, reading architecture as collectible images became a fetish only recognizable if such images were codifiable, if the images could he seen visually to belong to the set of expected images. The photograph tempts yet again an optical truth.

More recently, editors have begun to realize that the urgency is elsewhere. The packaged presentation of revealed details and the mass and balance of a revealed structure seem less significant than chance details. Huxtable is right. Serial, not static, events are virtually unphotographable, just as unphotographable we might say as Le Corbusier's Mill Owners' building in Ahmedabad or the Carpenter Centre. However, new developments in photography are around. Even a fresh architectural adventure and a new sort of architectural narrative looks as though it might finally be peopled by the architectural photographer's loathing—people themselves. The architectural photograph will then operate as its own photojournalism.

Fredric Jameson asked what that appetite for architecture was that has been revived by postmodernism. "I think it is the appetite for photography," Jameson answered himself. In fact, he might easily have identified an appetite for consumption, for this is what he seeks himself in the architecture: "What we want to consume today are not the buildings themselves, which you scarcely even recognize as you round the freeway." Though Jameson does acknowledge that many are the postmodern buildings that seem to have been designed for photography, I think we would have to disagree with his conclusion: "It is the value of the photographic equipment you consume first and foremost, and not of its objects."[22] Surely it is not the value of the equipment anymore; equipment is, after all, with the camera, the handy-cam, the egg-cam and digital editing world, literally disposable. Is it not the consumption of the building itself as a manipulatable image in the collectible set? Is it not part of the theater of architectural images that appealed so much and surprisingly still appeals? Architecture beyond the reality of controlled and manipulated production is still a game of recognition and belonging, a game that journalism and publishing have fostered.

Encouraged by sophisticated and relentless cataloging, postmodernism is not the sole property of literary critics. In fact, it may not be the property of literary critics at all, for they have, as we know, shifted allegiance. The altering canon moves on, re interpreted through negation, critical schemata, and the emergence of newer language.

The architectural coding game chanced its own significance, and for a time in the 1980s some felt it had achieved that reluctant but desirable public coding truthfulness for architecture.

It did not hold. Trainspotting took over once more, the voodoo came up. As Jameson described: "Tout, au monde, existe pour aboutir au Livre"—everything in the world exists to be brought to book. "Well," Jameson emphasizes, as if catching the crime in the phrase "brought to book," "at least the picture book, and many are the postmodern buildings that seemed to have been designed for photography."

"Brought to book" is indeed a useful English idiom for our purpose here. Rounding up the usual suspects, postmodernism surely has no privilege in photography's lament, just as it has no privilege in the dissolution of the inside and the outside. Modernism, for example, has always remained within the surface of its own event. It has been photographed and visually orchestrated to encourage if not coerce an accepted, harmonious flow of the "modern image." A fake history of modern architecture can be seen to lead to a fake history of the last century. The collected and collated images appear time and time again, reinforcing each other. Within a world on strict picture-search, it is obvious that many buildings do not conform to an accepted image. Competitions reinforce this (non)-conformity. Nor is it unreasonable wisdom to note that some buildings are of a type that clearly do not suit any comfortable notions of photography. Of course, serious architecture survives such loss. But there is real triumph here for an architecture inaccessible to the camera, inaccessible to surveillance and control. It is triumph, too, for an architecture that prevents the formulation of any complete picture, an architecture that, and Jameson exaggerates slightly, "recognises a freshness of experience from the habituated and reified numbness of everyday life in the fallen world." Quite how this triumph of an incomplete architecture is stretched to match his claim is unclear. Suddenly language scaffolds what we cannot photograph, what we think we cannot communicate. Big questions take over, questions which leave us uncertain whether photography or even architecture are ever likely to answer unequivocally. And just as suddenly, we lose hold on architecture again because of its very exaggeration. The voodoo rises!

Despite this, one of the clear gains of much contemporary architecture will be its evasion of the neat and acceptable architectural photograph. Future architecture may also prove, against the odds, to be remarkably sane in maintaining space and line. The architectural photograph, for example, rarely tells us the following: the building is an open form, not closed. The photograph does not tell us this: in movement its solidity of material and culture remain unfinished, incomplete The photograph does not tell us that the building was a complex stunning space in its neo-modernist underclothes of raw concrete and is now a touch too polished. The photograph will not tell why now, in its pristine white dress, this particular architecture is strangely remarkable, yet unapproachable. Nor will the photography tell us that this is an architecture that will mature when its "ruination" begins. Neither will the photograph tell us when the building and space will look lived-in. The photograph does not choose the word "sleekly handsome" or "dizzily angled." So how do we know to which architecture to apply such phrases?

The very real questioning and interrogations within the architectural experience and its pact with photography are surely never more than a reformulation of the expected. For at least three decades now, a neutral photography opting for the pretense of critical openness and freshness can be seen to have failed much contemporary architecture. If this is a talent at missing the point of critical inquiry itself, the architectural culture may be depriving itself of that most important critical tool for any development—self-criticism. In this case, when the carnival is over, after the voodoo hangs there, the photograph hijacks seduction and operates where language is impoverished.

There may be a fraudulence in some contemporary architecture that is hard to describe but which times itself to safety. Saying this might allow the sand timer to settle, but a more interesting debate arises. Loaning the privilege of modernism's promise, how much does photography need to reformulate architecture's own position in the international scene and in history? Today, when generations are growing up with MTV in their veins and paper clip and neon flattened cat installations fill the art galleries, impossible architecture evading photography might redirect the appetite for architecture away from optical truths and eternal metaphysical gaming. And as to the cultural logic of late capitalism, the architect also hasn't fared too well. For photography and a surviving view of the architect as the "Last Action Hero," we'd do better consulting Joseph Brodsky than Fredric Jameson.

Architects, scumbags, and the luftwaffe might seem an odd way to bring in photography. In his novel *Watermark,* Joseph Brodsky discusses a woman he meets in Venice. He is introduced to both the woman's sister and the woman's husband.

After meeting the husband, Brodsky finds what some may think a rather unusual reason for cuckoldry: her husband is an architect. We are left in no doubt about the currency of the profession: "The latter, whose appearance completely escapes my memory for reasons of redundancy, was a scumbag of an architect, of that ghastly post-war persuasion that has done more harm to the European skyline than any luftwaffe."[23]

This is apparently a rather wide opinion, one that we cannot lay to rest by merely blaming the critic Charles Jencks for a montage of modernist tower blocks and luftwaffe air raids. Though he did introduce the theme in his film *Kings of Infinite Space*, with the luftwaffe choreographed to destroy London, it has become a generally accessible, populist charge—the architect more dangerous than the luftwaffe! The relative cheapness of this idea does not hide the weight of emotion against architects, held especially in the latter part of the twentieth century. The weight of Prince Charles's commitment to architecture in the 1980s in Britain was steadied by similar emotion, to the extent that it became hard to convince the public that the twentieth century had not failed its architectural mission, that "modernism" itself must start over.

Brodsky continues his story of the architect: "In Venice, he defiled a couple of wonderful campi with his edifices, one of which was naturally a bank, since this sort of human animal loves a bank with the longing of an effect for its cause." Bank, corporate center, insurance headquarters, museum— you name it, and they can mirror emptiness as well as opulence. Brodsky is merciless, and if this had been a novel and not stylized mémoire, no doubt the husband would have been cuckholded. "For that 'structure' (as they called it in those days) alone, I thought he should be cuckholded. But since, like his wife, he, too, seemed to be a member of the CP, the job, I concluded, was best left to a comrade."

Certainly the job might be best left to the comrades if any can be found to own up to such delinquency. Brodsky nicely rounds off his story leaving us once more in no doubt about his determination to rid Venice, if not the world, of this loathsome breed:

Fastidiousness was part of it, the other part was that when, somewhat later, I called the only-person-I-knew-in-that-city from the depths of my labyrinth one blue evening, the architect, perhaps sensing in my broken Italian something untoward, cut the thread. So now it was really up to our red Armenian brethren.

The outrage against architects and architecture is almost everywhere and too easy, and it is certainly likely to continue in this new century. In an article in the *Observer* about the Millennium Festival in Greenwich we are left in no doubt about the status of architecture and the value of the architect's vision:

The site might be swimming in toxic sludge, the Tube link may not be finished and the entire city of Birmingham might be threatening to boycott the event out of pique, but the Millennium Festival at Greenwich finally looks as though it could, after all, prove to be a success—for one simple reason. It will allow us all to be delightfully rude, again, about architects.[24]

This is dismal appreciation: wit only hiding more frustration and bewilderment.

The rudeness against architects needs more talent than we often have available to us. Professional and political distrust have continually been asking for a reformulation in architecture. Such a reformulation that could at least take us away from the known and rather common attacks on architects might begin with rethinking the architectural photograph. Could we not more acknowledge the promises that cannot be performed within photography, as absurd as this may sound? Not all architecture from architects navigating philosophy to enlarge the construct of architecture itself can be dismissed as esoteric maneuvers. And not all these maneuvers are to be represented or damned by the photograph. Nor are all architects part of a coherent freemasonry supposedly controlling the dominant discourse(s). But if as much attention had been spent on the way images have been selected to accompany architectural argument and discourse, as it has been spent on the language used within architecture, distrust would be lessened, if not relieved. Altering architecture, given the contradictions inherent in the profession and the difficulty of remaining credible—socially and ethically, politically and economically—is not as difficult as is continually made out. Nor is it so clear that architecture itself is best functioning as an abstract critical tool, a social register and a cultural attitude. Would it not be urgent to alter the paradigms for reading architecture, if architecture continues being reduced to a compromised practice, while awarding brilliant philosophies of inaction to the world's leading architects?

It would also be just as urgent to understand how photography has played its own archival and ideological role in architecture's "dismay." Altering the way we read architecture, which includes the way photography informs and deforms architectural promise, would help us understand why contemporary architecture is considered inactive and incomprehensible to all but architects themselves. More radical under these unstable conditions, freed of its absurd involvement in simplistic communication, ravished but ecstatic, architecture could be heading toward a dissemination, a dispersal of a much rawer productive power. Rethinking the architectural photograph might accelerate such a speculation. We need to reemphasize: a state in which we are no longer able to stabilize meaning need not be as uncertain as we imagine or fear. Paralleling the poststructural exercise some want to tie it too, architecture of such rawness becomes an unfolding of pure exteriority, folds in a singular reality. This is also Beckett's "simple relief of the self-cancellation, there in the bull, at one with the complicated blasphemy."[25]

Literature needs no authenticity. "Just as in dress," Michel de Montaigne writes, "any attempt to make oneself conspicuous by adopting some peculiar and unusual fashions is the sign of a simple mind." Architectural photography, like architectural jargon, has not yet caused the embarrassment it should have. Montaigne continues: "So in language, the quest for new-fangled phrases and little known words springs from a puerile and pedantic pretension. I wish that I could limit myself to the language of the Paris markets."[26]

The language of the Paris markets is as much Irish as the "bull." Our difficulty is immediate. How can we speak of an architecture in such abstract terms if it cannot hold itself to higher and lower claims? How can we see it as a coherent field of activity if it broke up the last century and did as much damage as the luftwaffe? How can we possibly see it in terms of its photographic as much as its philosophical limit?

In the case of early man, we can be sure that the more accu-

rately he drew his potential prey, the more he could be said

to 'know' the animal he was depicting. The more knowledge

he had, the more likely he was to be successful in the hunt.

—ANTHONY STORR[1]

There is a story about Alfred Hitchcock in 1944, during the
making of the film *Lifeboat*, starring William Bendix, Tallulah
Bankhead, and Walter Slezak. The film involved revelations
about shipwreck survivors adrift during World War II. With
the action out in mid-ocean Hitchcock, suddenly concerned,
turned to the composer of the film score and said: "Don't you
think the audience will wonder where the music comes from?"
The composer is known to have replied: "Don't you think the
audience will wonder where the cameras came from?"

Architecture begins to have the same concern. In the last
essay we identified some appetites and options on the interplay
between architecture and photography. Experiencing photography as represented architecture inevitably remains an experience of "delay." An intermediate realm leads us toward an
undoing, a possible choice to remain ignorant, if not ignorance
itself. Why should we be so disturbed if architecture attempts
to communicate through codes from other disciplines, codes
we struggle less and less to recognize? To take this intermediate
realm further and put it more dramatically in terms of the
Tibetan bardo, we might take a clue from Rod Mengham:
"The secret purpose of language may not be to further com-

munication between the living and the living, but between the living and the dead."[2] What if representation through photography helps architecture only as a form of memory between the living and the living, no further communication? More perhaps we should not attempt!

Laurence Sterne begins chapter 40 of his novel *Tristram Shandy* in the following way: "I am now beginning to get fairly into my work; and by the help of a vegetable diet, with a few of the cold seeds, I make no doubt but I shall be able to go on with my uncle Toby's story, and my own, in a tolerable straight line now."[3] Before this tolerable straight line, Sterne treats us to a diagrammatic view of his narrative progress in the novel. With all the talk of narrative and critical fictions, this century's architecture surely comes to mind when we see Sterne's four diagrams.

Dividing these diagrams into twenty-year periods offers us a guide to architecture's history for latecomers to the twentieth century. By necessity approximate, our interpretations are naturally rewritable according to the schemata and historical shape preferred. But the scribble nevertheless is worth interpreting. Sterne's first line could be seen as the period of futurism, from 1900 to 1920, now described in critical historical jargon as "Nothing of the Past Absolutism." The second line could represent the period of internationalism, from 1921 to 1940, referred to also as "Doctrinaire Functionalism and Repressed Pluralism." The third line, 1941 to 1960, can be seen as "modernism" now reformulated as "Contextualism and Dwindling Absolutism." And the fourth, from 1961 to 1980, that period known as postmodernism is already rescripted as "Neo-Historicism and Rampant Pluralism." The reformulations will

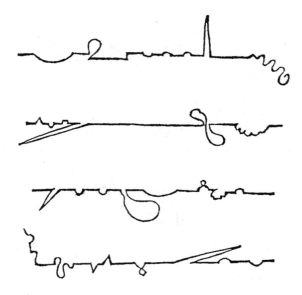

Drawings from Laurence Sterne's *Tristram Shandy* (London: Dent, 1967), p. 347.

continue, depending on which critical history we choose, but what then of the last twenty years, 1980 to 2000? If these four schemes can be taken as even general critical lines, it is rather obvious that in the last twenty-year period we have been presented with a much more erratic "narrative." The unassured pluralism of a late modernism gave way to runaway pluralism. "*The scene is polyglot,*" according to Heinrich Klotz,[4] one of the more open, indefatigable archivists of the century.

Returning to Sterne, however, it is the next drawn line that draws our interest. "In the fifth volume," Sterne goes on to write, "I have been very good,—the precise line I have described in it being this":

Drawing from Laurence Sterne's *Tristram Shandy* (London: Dent, 1967),
p. 347.

"The precise line," Sterne calls it. Just what is precise about
it is begged, as we would expect from Sterne. Is it the precision
of the drawn, the precision of the imagined, the precision of
the falsified? Or is it the precision of the uttered? Like the
choice of illustrative support in architectural publications and
histories, this is an obvious gesture of discrimination that we
hang on to before dying from laughter or stupidity. It is never
impartial. Let us continue by applying a little adventurous nar-
ratology to Sterne's fifth drawing before we arrive again at what
is apparent, the "gap."

What might that gentle curve be at the beginning of the
1980s, followed by a small star burst? Could it be the late
flowering of postmodernism so quickly flattening out into a
tired historicism, with a Catherine wheel explosion—the *B* in
Sterne's diagram—mid-1980s? Could this coincide with
Charles Jencks's elevation of Michael Graves' Portland Building (1982) into iconic status? Whatever the claims and coun-
terclaims during this period, exaggeration made sure that
an architectural confectionary spread. Architects were bitterly

divided by the Portland Building. Pastry cooks everywhere were impressed by the culinary and architectural crossover. Superchefs and architects from Delhi to Dallas realized that ideas for cuisine came as much from architectural orders as from vegetable diets. After the essays and publications, after the apotheosis of postmodernism and its public access to architecture through a nouvelle-piscine color coding, the narrative leveled out.[5]

Mid-1980s architecture took little frisks of digression. On its way a plateau evolved. Architecture developed into an antidoctrinaire theory ensuring that differing tendencies were accepted with comparative validity. General coding access meant that supermarkets could upstage star architects and star architects could downstage Athens and antiquity. The small chain of little *c*'s ran us, according to Jencks, out of the age of the proletariat and into the age of the cognitariat.[6] The only thing we were sure about was our ignorance; most of us never knew where the shoulder of the proletariat ended and the breast of the middle class began. Knowledge changed place with ignorance, invitations for the carnival were sent by courier with a Dire Straits sound track. In architecture, we were as far away as ever, with theory to scaffold our solitude.

Pastry cooks everywhere suddenly became aware of the trouble with double coding. Eclecticism is no natural style for culinary diversity anymore than a rampant relativism of the palate. Serious cooks were naturally suspicious of the shared symbolic order of the kind that a religion provides. For architecture without religion, Jencks insisted, the shared symbolic order was effected through a double coding, implicating more than irony in the architectural scheme. The result was a continual overreach for symbolism, meaning and continuity, a truthfulness splintering the coding "logic" as fast as it proposed itself as a reading model.

Iterative processes took over, informing the double code with absence, hurriedly turning back on architecture the codes that could be ironized. This tended to sabotage, as pastry cooks well knew, the destructions of value necessary to keep postmodernism postmodern. Lyotard was always going to be a more reliable source for this double backing, as relativism was condemned the closer it came to the circus of its own coding, double coding, and effacement. Hard to grasp but so easily diluted, so various in style, postmodernism's unruly coherence and discontinuity were only answered, sadly, by the correctness of the rupture. Later, Jencks was to graft the whole nonlinear worldview onto an architecture, making present once more what deconstruction tempted to remain absent. Enter the butterfly and morphogenesis, pause for the "swirl," the fractal flourish of the entrance gates to heaven's distillery.

There is no original point of departure for any architecture trying to efface what went before. To respond to the present, to make a fiction of the present from the past or seek a nostalgia for the future always begins with an informative, iterative process. Success depends on how well this is masked. The access to hallucinatory coherence makes all the differance.[7] The architectural archive represented by Jencks's inimitable and engaging mapping was ahead of us all. It had already been prepared for the carnival takeover. Jargonauts were more popular than cosmonauts. Architecture went public, floated as it was on a market bed of seduction and favor. During this period, drawings joined photography and elevated the mystical role of the architectural publication. I publish, therefore I am (an architect) became more than understandable.

In an astute essay, "Architecture and Its Image," Helen Lipstadt attempts a definition of architectural publication. She describes the process clearly in a discussion of the concept of figuration:

Figurations that circulate as (relatively) pure cultural goods outside the building process, figurations that have "gone public" are "publications." Derived from any part of the practice of architecture, they begin their lives within the evolution or space from conception to construction and escape from that process into the world of architectural culture, achieving, either permanently or momentarily, the status of (relatively) independent cultural goods.[8]

Representation for publication not only merited special attention during this plateau time, but in fact took over as a narrative of representation for architecture. If it became superfluous to fall back on the past, it was not superfluous to fall back on language and the lexicographer's art. And the architects had it both ways, as Edward Robbins captures it: "If those who are not architects are forced to work through their ideas within a form of discourse that is the architect's, then it is the architect's vision that in the final analysis is dominant."[9]

The compiling of architectural narrative and history, using photograph, drawing, and scaffolded texts, entailed an exercise of immense scale and, let us be clear about it, an obvious ambiguity about the social control and cultural production of architecture. As Colomina suggests, overlapping systems of representation not always making their "presence" felt, should shift our consideration to representation itself:

To think about (modern) architecture must be to pass back and forth between the question of space and the question of representation. Indeed, it will be necessary to think of an architecture as a system of representation, or rather a series of overlapping systems of representation. This does not mean abandoning the traditional architectural object, the building. In the end, it means looking at it much more closely than before, but also in a different way. The building should be understood in the same terms as drawings, photographs, writing, films, and advertisements; not only because these are the media in which more often we encounter it, but because the building is a mechanism of representation."[10]

The mechanics of architectural representation are beginning to rebound on us. As encyclopedias and universal dictionaries of architecture become sacred guardians of architecture's cultural traditions, buildings get further away from the drawn, the photographed, the filmed, and the advertised. The "gap" widens into a nervous bardo; the paradoxical *bulls* presented for architectural scholarship could not be clearer. Rampant archiving happened at precisely the same time when cultural conventions (film, photography, drawing, language, and advertising) were being attacked and reformulated. It was a time when the instability in language and philosophy carnivalized the archive itself. As architecture cataloged itself to a flat-earth death, literature and philosophy departments were doing their best to dismantle the art of the lexicographer.

For convenient arrest, let us try to trace this trajectory back
to Sterne's fifth diagram. The little c's advanced, suggesting
that change was necessary to the normative idealism of modernism and runaway historicism. Everyone was doing it, everyone was underground, traveling on the Circle Line, yet
something was needed, something outside architecture, to
bury postmodernism. Or so it was felt in the precise inexactitude that passed for critical scholarship. Something that validated plurality and ambiguity, reformulated the past without
worship and was already pricking other disciplines, was necessary. Thus, a movement that validated plurality and ambiguity,
reformulating the past without worship, was discovered to be
waiting—like Monsieur Godot—in the wings of the architectural theater. It was only at the large blowout, or apparition
marked D on Sterne's diagram, that we can now appreciate
what happened. Deconstruction punctured the narrative.

The ease with which deconstruction could work in a back-
ground of tired neo-historicism is now recognized. Its emphasis on philosophical undoing might parallel modernism's
early dependence on loose linguistic theories, objective truth
scenarios, and simplified communication theory. Flattening
out into star burst and plateau, the iconic "playback" language of modernism (suprematism/constructivism/de Stijl/fu-
turism/cubism) became a part of the syntax and memetics
of a normative visual deconstruction. As is often the case,
latecomers hijacked the exercise and entered with their own
"dazzling images." To echo Sterne and to believe others, deconstruction has not only led architecture around the houses
but it has done the (necessary) devil's work. More than this
merry dance, useful as a ladder up which to climb, deconstruc-

From Laurence Sterne's *Tristram Shandy* (London: Dent, 1967), p. 347.

tion itself had to be disgarded, undone, in order finally to clear us of such detritus. This is not a long way from what the devils did to Sterne in his novel. Finally, as the little row of lowercase *c*'s vanish into nothing, we have to leave the question as to whether they are nothing more than mere transgressions of architecture's firmer path.[11] If so, we would be left with *A, B,* and *D.* And as if to anticipate our anxiety, to aid us to complete our unending narrative, Sterne ends his diagram with the flourish. A flourish? A swirl? From an eighteenth-century English novel and all manufactured, overread, from a simple diagram! What voodoo is this now? But this is a swirl, a musical hint, a digression, far from redundant. Let it remain as another warning against ourselves as we now get endless versions of the twentieth century, rewritten and repackaged for architectural publication. It is difficult not to see this swirl of the fencer's art as the abyss or the creative gap we are now presented with. More importantly, the gentle gap must now surely open up. If we are right and language—more properly an applied linguistics—has attempted to make of architectural codes a legibility all its own, then it is drawing and the drawn that ensures a continued ambiguity as to the point of departure for architectural vision.

The "point of departure," like the aphorism, has long tried to support the whole architectural process. And like the aphorism, all hidden insight within such drawings might fail ultimately against the silent articulation of architecture itself. Did architecture need a philosopher like Jacques Derrida to tell it this? For Derrida must have known well enough, as architecture began hijacking philosophy, that conflicts and contest would arise. Architects would be dead meat when architectural theory began insinuating itself in philosophy's territory. What no one knew, and perhaps still does not know, is how much this gap would open up, how liberating the bardo could be when philosophy itself starting staking itself out on architectural ground.[12]

An aphorism is a precept or principle, Webster's tells us, expressed in a few words—an axiom, maxim, or adage. Aphorisms have been a favored tactic of architects more so than critics or commentators. Deep or facile brevity obviously attracts the practitioner. Aphorisms are a type of defensible archobabble. Mies van der Rohe used them. Kahn used them. Corb used them. Aalto used them. Johnson uses them. Rogers uses them. Foster uses them. Eisenman uses them. Any talk of salmon, a trout, or a flounder crossed with a useful stream or brook, or talk of a shaft of pagan light invites any number of architectural interpretations and astonishment. But *"bulled"* as we have become through endless paradoxes in architectural scheming, coded as we are for any meaningful interaction, we are not quite as meaningless as we think. If only we were confused all the time, Sogyal Rinpoche suggests, that would at least make for some kind of clarity.[13]

There is so obviously a seductive ease in the architectural aphorism attracting us by its limited silence. And though the aphorism might be close to being as redundant as possible, usually an aphorism does not, should not, or cannot, tell us quite as much about architecture as a drawing. "For if there is a truth in architecture," Derrida claims, "it appears doubly allergic to the aphorism." We could say the same of the drawing. Essentially, Derrida explains, the truth of architecture occurs outside of discourse.

There has been no mistaking it. Over the last twenty years this has been the biggest alibi for architectural metaphysics and voodoo. Contributing to the essential art of inexactitude, this "aphorism" has been spoken out and was up and running before symposiums blinked. Everyone was caught up with it soon enough—directly or indirectly—as language became the scaffold in architectural discourse from New York to New Delhi. But if that was philosophy's Big One, there was an even bigger one waiting. And whole auditoriums were caught looking the wrong way, whole colloquys. Though architecture concerns an articulated organization, it is but silent. Or then mute! The chandeliers trembled. Derrida was being used and abused to tell grown-up architects precisely what Antoine St. Exupéry told them in his book *The Little Prince*. Architects need the retelling. Interpreted differently for architecture's own flattened response, it meant the obvious for architecture: the drawing as a container for all, redundant, mute, full of anomaly, social control, essential congruity and real incongruity. Such (a) contradictory compacting is what animates both blasphemy and the bull.[14] As an animation both blasphemic and bullish, I propose to take a look at what became one of the

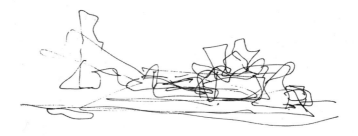

Frank Gehry, 1992, concept sketch of the Guggenheim Museum, Bilbao.
© 1995 Solomon R. Guggenheim Foundation.

most published scribbles of the last decade of the twentieth
century. This is Frank Gehry's point-of-departure scribble for
The Bilbao Guggenheim Museum.

Seen as an aphorism from the other side of architecture, it
should not be difficult to think of this drawing as hieroglyphic.
Modern research has updated Herodotus, the Greek historian.
Three systems are considered in operation within Egyptian
writing: hieroglyphic, which is sacred; hieratic, which is
priestly; and demotic, which is popular. Sacred, priestly, and
popular, the highly formal aspect of the hieroglyph is adapted
and abbreviated as it needs to pass from stone to more perishable materials. This act is reversed in the architectural drawing.
The visualization of architectural thought, the relationship of
the ideal to the material, and the mechanics of production
take an opposite course. The drawing is perishable clearly but
priestly. It only passes to the third stage when it is published
and becomes "demotic." It merits special attention in its place
and publication and becomes "popular."

In his compilation *Why Architects Draw,* Edward Robbins
has described the various uses drawings can be put to in archi-

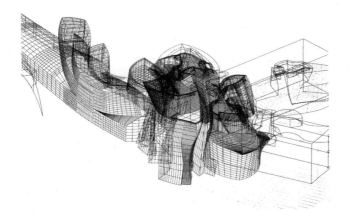

Frank Gehry, CATIA wire-frame model of the Guggenheim Museum, Bilbao, 1995. Frank Gehry & Associates. © 1995 Solomon R. Guggenheim Foundation.

tectural production: "As an agenda and a mnemonic, a form of dialogue as well as a visual guideline, the drawing serves as both the subject of conversation and the object of our endeavors."[15] Though Robbins well catalogs the stages of the drawing in architectural production and the ultimate control of production the architects seek, this is not quite our concern here. For us the mnemonic is likely to be replaced by the demonic. Gehry's "scrawl" is a cursive script, the scratchings of a running hand. We imagine it done at speed, at the dinner table or the drawing board. We imagine it disposable, as on an airplane with the free nightpack, or then a champagne-before-take-off drawing!

"I'm looking through the paper to try to pull out the formal idea," Gehry says, "it's like somebody drowning in paper."[16]

And that's why we, like Gehry, are invited not to think of
them merely as drawings. Moving rapidly, the hand joins sepa-
rate strokes together and takes the drawing into a vulgar form
where any instrument could serve for this representaton: Biro,
felt pen, ink, pencil. The "departure" drawing preserves a notion of authorship, or so we think. As Coosje van Bruggen
describes: "Gehry shifts from being the author engaged in his
semiautomatic scrawling/writing to assuming the role of the
investigative reader ready to disentangle potential forms enmeshed within the multiple lines and contours caught in his
drawings."[17] This authorship then blurs as the scribbles pass
over to finer detail, measured drawings, the architectural production of a bureau including blue-line prints, or, in Gehry's
case, the sophisticated and orchestrated computer-aided design
(Catia) drawings.

Sometimes it is hard to imagine that there is any link between these enmeshed and enmeshing scribbled lines and the
reality in built form. Is architecture really outside everything
that attempts to describe it, even a scrawl that attempts not
to hold it back? Gehry's realization of the building from such
scratchings is not, however, secondary to the concept enmeshed within the lines. The reader may be the redeemer of
built redundancy, but it needs the multiplicity of Gehry to
unravel the near "nonsense" of a scrawl into the finished building: "Drawing is a tool," Gehry says. "So is the model. Everything is a tool. The building is the only thing that means
anything—the finished building."[18] Neither does the scrawl
seem to overpropagandize for Gehry's own aesthetic strategy,
though many see this as an astute public relations exercise. But
how such scratching is the perfect instrument or tool for a

transformation into communicable architecture is beyond the sketch. This is *The Little Prince* dilemma that we see emerge later.

There has always been an enigma in the departure of architectural thought. If not private, intuitive, chance gestalt, it is public, ordered, rational, and accessible. Or so such dualism was considered to exist. Things could change, though, forever with the introduction of infinite digital modeling into architectural production. Alteration, less unstable than we imagined, could become a permanent strategy as software becomes more accessible, more manipulative. Before this erases any astonishment at departure for architectural idea and form, let us, however, consider the more conventional "departure" of drawings.

Drawings can act as aphorisms when they operate as a precept or principle briefly expressed. This is precisely what they are: something expressed briefly. The few words of an aphorism can become, in the architect's drawing, axiomatic. They can also become idiomatic. When we speak of the idiomatic we can speak of the recognition within which appears a scribble of lines of an architecture. This should not be confused with the "signatorial." To speak of a signature in architecture has been and continues to be misleading. Gehry's signature differs from Aalto's, Mies's differs from Kahn's, Eisenman's from Tschumi's, Gehry's from Libeskind's, etc. This is flat-earth coding, unhelpful, as the word *signature* is merely used as a short-circuit to the visually recognizable, critical convenience of certain architects. It encourages reading architecture backward toward familiarity.

Yet when faced with sketches and drawings, how is it possible—as critics, commentators, and historians—to organize our approach? How can we formulate this encounter? How can we look at the drawing and say, We know where you are coming from? Where, for example, is the morphology in Gehry's sketch that we know can take on an endless variety of shifting forms and move from the balancing act to a composition? Is there not in any scribble, even from a child, or a smudge from the thumb or a Rorschach ink test basically an endless variety of shifting forms? In ancient Egypt the image was believed to guarantee some sort of survival after death. If the sculptor was known as he-who-keeps-alive, then what of the architect: he-who-remains-alive?[19]

In Cyra McFadden's novel *The Serial,* we continually meet the phrase, "I know where you're coming from." By using this coded utterance a speaker indicates some access to a person's past, some familiarity with the conditions through which they have lived and some understanding of the circumstances of their life. In other words, we have an understanding of the context of their lives. Or we think we have. Thus, "I know where you're coming from" can mean: I understand, though I may not agree with you, why you said what you said or why you did what you just did. Set in Marin County on the West Coast of America, we see this piece of psychobabble operate as apology, cliché, therapy, terrorism, and tolerance. Woody Allen has turned film around from such (im)potential dialogue. Sharing with the aphorism, this is the wink-wink world coded for a meaningful interaction that has become meaningless, but not, clearly, redundant.

A drawing operating as an aphorism usually cannot tell us quite as much. Yet how and why do we continue to try to mine them for their architectural achievement and intention? Why do we make from all types of architectural drawings supports for a didactic process? And just how can we tell if and when the images function independently of any observed reality or their own intention? Current publications exhaustively presenting the drawing might be inadvertantly leading architecture toward the redundancy of such drawn representation. Unable to signify, the drawings begin to operate as mute indicators of what architecture should look like instead of, according to Lebbeus Woods, imagining that what is made now has always been.

Further, published drawings have long begun to operate as indicators of how architecture "ought to be" drawn, ought to be possible. Serving the politician, the cultural administrator, and the weekend supplement reader, these become membership games. Such games and implicit codes of representation take us even further away from the usual consumer of architecture, who would in all likelihood have to turn to Piaget for a guide to the hidden insight into the childlike line and play. As if to raise the stakes of secrecy and privilege, the architectural notebook is idealized and the restaurant cuff-sketch idolized.

Clearly, criticial "gaming" has had its consequence in the drawn too. When attempts are being made for an architecture beyond a priori signification, an architecture problematizing meaning, the *counter-écriture* or the "signifiant sans signifié" of Roland Barthes are no longer remote from architectural "departure." Whether a Barthes "scribble" is idle or not no longer matters. The imagined building, an architectural projection, or a constructed word, can be within or without. Deconstruct and then add fictional content and functional dream, compositonal refinement and aesthetic irritant, and the scribble is potential software for a building of incomparable architectural vision. Repression will see to the parts ordinary programs never reach. In the hidden narrative the strokes search for meaning, daggers![20] Add metaphor and metaphysical scheming to Barthes's drawn "nothing," add the hieroglyphic, the hieratic, and the demotic, and we would have an architectural production. A production of splinters, shot through with shards, legitimated by hazy visions, lost traces and a whole host of poststructural ballast and software morphing; a building would have to emerge. We could use Huxtable's words about Zaha Hadid's Vitra Fire Station: "sleekly handsome, dizzily angled." A fire station, a gallery, an edge project, or a bank?

Doing this, gaming so with repression and line does not make the scribble invalid as a departure for architecture. Vocabulary can be reapplied. And vocabulary can always redescribe the lost in order to appear found. This should not be difficult to follow after all the literary sorties into architectual validity of the last thirty years. If the fiction of architecture has narrowed out then it is also surely not difficult to bring it back. But how, in an era of continuous validity and invalidity, in an era of thrilling contest, do such drawings work on us?

The drawings—a priori and a posteriori—are both confounded by publication. Any sketch of a salmon, any shaft of pagan light, invites any number of architectural departures.

Roland Barthes, *Doodling . . . or the signifier without the signified,* from
Roland Barthes by Roland Barthes (New York: Hill and Wang, 1977),
p. 187. Reprinted by permission of Macmillan Ltd. and Michel Salzedo.

Any amount of cool waves in oxidized steel have any amount
of poetic resonance. Yet if the drawing is even more ambiguous
than that, surely it begs a much bigger question: after all this
fiddle, after all the archiving of the late twentieth century, are
we sure architecture is, or should be, decodable at all? *Signifiant
sans signifié?*

I suggest we go local to go universal, and consider the
series of drawings by the Finnish architect Reima Pietilä,
which went to make up the official residence of the president of Finland, Mäntyniemi, in Helsinki (1993). How, for
example, might we expect the drawing—aphoristically—to
speak of Finland? Would it not help in architectural thinking and in terms of "departure" if we knew where each of
us were coming from? Would it help if we had a glimpse,
however brief, of the motives behind the draughtsman's
contract?[21]

Pietilä, like many carefully ambiguous architects, incessantly raids his own departure. It is a form of writing that
balloons out from the gestalt sketch. Like many architects, he
also had the desire to monitor his own draughtsman's contract.
It is as if he wanted to be there—wherever "there" was—
before someone else could be. And like many practititoners,
Alvar Aalto included, he could see more in the drawing than
the built work. Before we romanticize this process, there is also
a tragic side to this architectural self-monitoring. Often the
most radical project, the project in between all disciplines and
architecture, the project in the "gap," is never built.

In a rare exercise, a "bullish" tactic, confusing the a priori
and a posteriori, Pietilä prepared a catalog of the sketching and
drawing itinerary for the Finnish president's residence. One
doesn't know whether to forgive the architect for overtrying
or applaud the architect for offering explanations where some
are obviously not needed. After this diagrammatic mapping of
the drawings' critical path and options, and the architecture
so unintentionally formalized, do we imagine there to be a
tolerable straight line? Isn't Pietilä merely doing in this list
what Laurence Sterne sketched in his novel, with all the humor
intended?

1. Looking at scenery, clouds, trees, water, stones, sites at
Hankasalmi on the east and west border of Finland, between
Savo and Hame.
2. Contemplating Finnish morphology.
3. Making imaginary sketches of the terminal moraine of a
glacial flow.
4. Watching a film about Alaska's melting ice dams on TV.

5. Expressing the landscape object, image, and material for the project. An abandoned idea from an earlier project, its ice architecture, flashes through the mind.

6. Initial images of spatial movements.

7. Motion event, spacial characteristic, and outline of the focal interior.

8. Functions as metabolic sketches (1/500, colored felt pen).

9. Intermediate stage: forest space—interior space. Window prototype sketching.

10. Metabolic function sketches firmed up (1/500 colored felt pen).

11. Felt-pen space and line rhythms developed.

12. Overlaying of tracing paper; first "ruler" lines—plotting spatial intersecting lines. (1/100 felt pen—3B pencil).

13. Final floor plan (F pencil).

14. Elevations and sections.

15. The project is completed in collaboration with the office.[22]

Pietilä was a master of knowing when to leave language lying in the corridor. He also knew just when to put the tongue away and let the ambiguity of the drawing lead to an architecture he already envisioned long past. He shared this with Gehry and many other contemporaries. Fond of explaining and reexplaining, Pietilä, though, was a veritable Little Prince. Untiring and indefatigable, instead of becoming a pilot, he gave up a career in philosophy to explore through architecture what the last century seemed intent on failing to prove— whether architecture is reasonably metaphysical at all. The confidence of doubt and architectural contestation Pietilä brought to this debate would repay any scrutiny of his work today.

What of the drawings as points of departure and the route they take into predictable or unpredictable architecture? A computer modeling program would make the project seamless from the enigma of departure to the predictability of arrival. Of course, it is hard to tell whether Pietilä was applying—a posteriori—a knowledge of the architectural process into what seems like a foreknowledge about architectural emergence. This hardly matters. More intriguing with such architects is the chance insight, the chance way the architect allows impulses to shape the vision seen hazily but "perfectly" in advance. It is not a paradox, no more than Gehry's continual alterations, to find a form that he thinks intuitively was there at the beginning but needs mystery and chance, possibly some champagne, to reveal it.

Like Laurence Sterne's writing, such architectural thinking and departure needs a control and lightness all its own. But this is not to be confused with the casual. This lightness is also why we can put architects like Gehry, Libeskind, Hejduk, Mendelsohn, Hecker, and Pietilä together. And why later architects like Koolhaas, Alsop, Tschumi, Herzog, de Meuron, Ito, and Torres Tur, among others, will shift architectural departure into a lightness all their own. Despite their differences and relations with the architectural contest, the bardo flourish is similar. How general such a self-monitored, cataloged journey is for architecture I would be reluctant to state. But it has relevance for the role of the drawing in architectural departure.

The scribble begins to operate as a fictional sketch for the project. Mnemonic and demotic, one or other of the sketches may finally be redundant to the finished work, but they are never futile. The sketch is a trace (something that previously exists), a picaresque form, visited, learned from, and often abandoned along the way on the journey. Pietilä and Gehry speak of the sketch development as Sterne might speak about one of his chapters. And clearly before any one sketch appears as the iconic "first" sketch, the architectural process has begun way way back.[23] It is significant that the first five processes cataloged by Pietilä are continuous acts, modalities if you prefer: Looking, observing, making, watching, and express-ing. Like Gehry's Disney Auditorium, the Vitra Furniture Museum, the American Center or Bilbao's Guggenheim Mu-seum, the first sketch is cursive, freeflow, running, and—to many—demotic. These are scribbles. Fast-forwarded they be-come architecture. The "gap" is usually less mystery but more production, control, predictability, and not a small amount of luck.

In understanding the enigma of all departure, how far away are we from Rilke? "No, it is really better to draw, anything at all. In time the resemblance will appear. And art, when you acquire it this way, little by little, is after all something truly enviable."[24] Rilke knew full well that resemblance will appear and that it takes real talent to miss the point of resemblance. The way the scribble becomes architecture is a poetics from drawing to drawing, from fiction to fiction, and, in many ways, resembles the detective story in reverse. The architect builds up clues to the project, layer upon layer, and seems to make the final project more complex, possibly more difficult. At the same time as there are more and more clues to the eventual

form, the project becomes clearer and lucid. The bardo tri-
umphs. The victim of the crime, the mystery, is solved. Claims
of a wilful spontaneity about such architecture are usually hasty
and misplaced. Such "detecting" poetics are not random,
though the chance trace for the journey may seem to be. These
architects share contest and rigor. Theirs is not a solemn echo
to previous projects but a poetics always on the edge. It is this
which obviously presents the difficulty that many contemporary works display, and which many of the public refuse to
consider as architecture. What confuses the public, and you
can have some sympathy, is the way these architects can swerve
so perpetually. These are the architects that can be seen to be
widening, by their drawing and architecture, a repertoire that
does not easily fit in with current architectural language.

Architecture, where traces as different as Jewish history, the
Disney underworld, and a television program can recall, mirror, refine, kick-start, and then rework previous architectural
traces, have little precedence. Like Herzog and de Meuron,
who may not know what sort of architecture they are going
to do on Monday morning, one guesses that they have something in mind. Unsurprisingly, the public, however, is out in
the cold. The public has yet to be convinced about the attraction of the incomplete in modernism, so how can their
support be expected for more and more contest, more and
more unrest in contemporary architecture?

The attraction of the imprecise was long assumed present
in the late-twentieth-century mind before the "undecidables"
overtook architectural philosophy. But some have raced on.
The hazy, the lost, the indistinct, the impossible, all bulls, all
redeemable by bardo thinking, are also retrieved by drawing,

just as Michel Foucault wrote about Raymond Roussell: "The gracefulness of the language . . . was that it gave the minuscule, the hazy, the lost, the poorly placed, the almost imperceptible (and even the most secret thought) with the same clarity as the visible.[25] This is a hard though challenging contract for anyone, asking the imperceptible to share the same clarity as the visible and making architecture from it. Blasphemy and the bull, a few black smudges, John Ashbery also tells us, can be a darkness all it's own, and the tragic side is always present in the hypnotic pull of using architecture as a ride to the other side.

A few black smudges
on the outer boulevards, like smashed midges
And the truth becomes a hole, something one has always known
A heaviness in the trees, and no one can say
where it comes from, or how long it will stay

A randomness, a darkness of one's own.[26]

There are clues in a drawing's own darkness, which manage to hide their own visibility. Gehry's scratchings do not really reveal. There is no key except for its role as scribble. Have we been right all along to assume that there should be clear routes and pointers from the trace and departure of an idea to the final project? Are we always so dismally disappointed if we are not allowed in? And why should we need ways into architectural thought if we are offered architecture that problematizes meaning and that process of thought itself? Why should we bother if the architectural thought dwindles in significance as we are able to experience something beyond this critical thought in the architecture itself? We know, if we follow Jacques Guillerme, that "figuration" means that the training of hand, eye, and mind makes the architect present as the defining characteristic. The Death of the Author has made no inroads here. In defining *figuration* in architectural representation, Guillerme puts it in a language we just about hold on to: "These activities are conceivable, however, only because his own body (the architect's) is involved in the operation of establishing difference in a scalar manner."

If only theoreticians would write like Sterne and give us some breathing space. Although we would probably prefer a swerve, a flourish or a pause, Guillerme continues, "The architect's body is an instrument whose role is to organize the distances between different spaces placed in imaginary correlations with each other."[27] Is it just me that has no longer the patience to negotiate or excavate such language? Or does it take a delinquent mind to think the undoing goes too far? We may scream for a logic of the hazy, the indistinct, but we also want that logic to be the occasion of an architecture ethically more than the subject. There is a crime about such language that makes it all so explicit but out of reach. Fashionable, it operates as sense and non-sense at the same time. So clear, so whole, so redundant, the architecture we are talking about then dances in between this language, as if dancing on a pyre. The architect, too, nods in agreement at the role of "figuration" in drawing, at the role of disjunction and ordinariness, but at the same time fakes it! We think the architect so engaged by maintaining a reference to construction, real or ideal, but in effect the architect whoops for joy at the idiocy of making it all fall for the rise of language itself. Can we not see and appreciate Etienne-Louis Boullée designing a cathedral for Paris and going ever so slightly over the top with those magnificent drawings? And can we not also warm to Boullée as he retrieves the megalomania by humor. In the middle of one of his drawings of the cathedral one can supposedly see a puppy. Like one of those 3-D drawings, you look and look until you go silly looking for the puppy. If we are not careful, we do the same with architecture!

Understanding where we are coming from can also inform us about what is being called conceptual leap frogging.[28] Before we too hastily blame other disciplines for architecture's own bypass maneuvers and conceptual shortcomings, let us digress slightly. During a critical review with students at the Belgrano University School of Architecture in Buenos Aires, the planning and rehabilitation of the Buenos Aires waterfront was under discussion. Three students, dressed impeccably and "loosely" in a happy-Monday black coding explained two projects. Both projects were conceptually bright, schematically even brilliant, so much so that we could speak of their aphoristic success as projects. If the models were more than competent, the drawings, graphically recognizable and contemporary, were uninspiring. Yet all was coded.

One scheme had Le Corbusian Marseille-Unité-Towers as a hotel area placed along the waterfront. That this might be a ghetto trapped in its own security and traffic congestion did not come up. The other project, a mega-scheme integrating culture with business, architecture as event and sequence, was located right on the edge of a reclaimed waterfront. Another ghetto suggested itself leaving the scheme a film-set fortress of no uncertain dimension. Both schemes suggested ambiguous high-rise futures, scenographic drama, and a possible instant gloomsville at night. The drawings were a rhetoric version of a J. G. Ballard novel. Perfectly coded, their schemes were schematically precise and superbly presented. Yet neither scheme passed over the thinness and immediacy of "representation," going into depth about transport, circulation, security, and the problematic spatial and formal movements across and through an area of a city. Familiar with magazines like *Interview, Arena, Wired, Wallpaper, Dutch,* and *Egoiste,* these schemes were cartoon-drawn, sound-bitten, resembling Schuiten's and Peeters's *La Fièvre d'Urbicande.*

Where were these students coming from? They certainly knew their William Gibson, but was this a new, ill-defined archobabble? *Neuromancers* all, the work was trapped in the brevity and brilliance of software and in response to the drawn project, an aphorism was all that presented itself. Aware of a complexity of space and reality, had these students forgotten their Ray Bradbury? Had they leapfrogged *Fahrenheit 451?* The most sordid signs for Jean Genet became signs of grandeur that obliquely remind us that the elevation of thinness is more than ever within our reach. A drawing, however unsignifying, can be opened up like a can of sardines. No textbook need tell us today that coded rhetoric and jargon can design architecture.

Recalling our idea of a world theater of architectural images, these students from Belgrano University come in somewhere after the novelist J. G. Ballard. On the scale of international imagery, they were locating architectural promise somewhere between a tired repetitive Peter Greenaway world and a Pet Shop Boys video. They would understand the slick graphics of a TV Dante but miss the *Inferno*. They would leapfrog into the graphics of a television film, morph everything but the girl, describe the postmodern world as "the real thing" but miss the backup. They listened to U2 and designed architecture that could step from cartoon image to cartoon image. Architectural relay this certainly produces, but is this not where all rogue architectural thinking begins, in a memetic displacement with our own pasts?

Saying that these students had forgotten their Bradbury means that their thinking was not just lost to a movement, scale, and understanding of an architecture and a city that we could witness in any science fiction from the 1950s. No, these students were coming from somewhere else. With their version of architecture, with their drawn worlds, they had leapfrogged into another "virtual reality." Harrison Ford designed their architecture, not Sean Connery. Architecture had cartoon and schematic potential; it was a graphic literalness, surface utopia wrapped in new material science. There, in front of our eyes, ambiguity was lost. The drawings had leapfrogged cartoon literature and schemed with philosophy and metaphor. No BBC World Service *Book-at-Bedtime* for these students, they read Derrida and Eisenman for dazzling rhetorical cribs and fugitive architectural scenarios. Admittedly, a "virtual architecture" was something that they were trying to talk about but for which, as a replication, had as yet no vocabulary.

One of the students asked about Peter Eisenman. I muttered something about bull-clever sliding and bardo liberation, something about syntax and "computer-mannerism" leveling off into a mature perpetually upset architecture! They looked through me as if I'd quantum leaped back to Kennedy's assassination or Woodstock! In private, in my own inner speech, which always goes on parallel with all outer events including this text, I thought of Heidegger: "The dreadful has already happened." One of the three appeared hurt, as if these comments were a personal insult against them and not Peter Eisenman. I meant neither. "But," he interrupted and explained eagerly, "the interesting thing about Eisenman is that it is all in his head."

To assess Eisenman for his computerized artifical intelligence didn't seem to me to be a particularly useful critical position to take in relation to Eisenman's more valid frontal attack on architectural thinking and convention. To continue Eisenman's own use of Baudrillard's language, it was undoubtedly a simulacrum that would not particularly flatter Eisenman. But we didn't go that far. The students smiled and asked another question: Do you know William Gibson? I smiled too, but did I really know where these students were coming from? Did I know William Gibson personally? Had I met Gibson? Had I read Gibson? Did I not know how Gibson could be applied to architecture? And so on.

Can I reasonably use this aphoristic jargon and gaming across time and literature with any understanding of the students' architectural thinking? What does it mean to say that the students knew their William Gibson, forgot their Ray Bradbury, and fell somewhere short of J. G. Ballard? Perhaps the clues come from Cyberia. "These kids are not only stealing information," Rushkoff writes, "they are surfing data." In relation to architecture, are these students so different? Can we not see architects no longer trawling but surfing (altering their metaphors to keep up with the surface of knowledge) through one system after another in order to put things and space together as never before?

To discover that secret room it may be that architects, too, are on a different frontier, where they evaluate so quickly the surface nature not only of their own information and creativity but of human relations. Fascinated by Sisyphus these students are not. For them, there may not exist any cul-de-sac of the sort we usually recognize in architecture, none of the lamentations of a tired twentieth-century brigade. Network is infinite, and so "what better language to adopt than computer language," as Rushkoff writes, ". . . unfettered by prejudices, judgments, and neurosis?"[29] The advantage, and it may be a large one, I heard them whisper, is the fact that the computer has no "interpretive" grid. Like the tripper once was, like the hitchhiker once was, like the hijacker once was, the surfer is: unprejudiced, aiming for that zero degree of interpretation.

Cyber personalities? Is that what we are faced with? Fractal fascination surfed onto architecture takes over just at the stage where previously the architect would normally look around and leave after discovering a dead end. Here there is no dead end. Visual experience is discontinuity defined from a limited angle. Feedback becomes second nature and iteration a daily fix. A darkness all our own making or out of our depth?

It is easy, though, and always has been, to have fun at architecture's expense through language. However immature these actions might have appeared, there was no mistakng the seriousness of the students. This was not a chance hobby but a construction for some sort of future. I had the feeling that these students would change the way the rest of us live without quite knowing about it, without us being able to do anything about it. I remembered a piece from Ballard and found it upon my return home: ". . . now nearing the end of the millennium, the steel towers, the fatigue steel structure allows the San Francisco Tower to reach up to God. But, the architect says, 'aesthetically, we do anything we want to do with technology.' "

This is an architectural mean, the simple relief of self-cancelation, like the words *improvisation, jazz, indeterminate architecture, undecidable form and brilliance, cusp,* and *transformation.* How do we use these words in a world receding from us? How many of us admit to a wounded half-poetic intellect? Personally, I can do no more than admit to innumerable hours spent dressing this wound in architecture. I participate in a grand thinking while the inner speech of another century, another world, is up there ahead of me. Only a grand innocence it seems can survive this redundancy. Our own innocence!

Much contemporary architecture is hopelessly defined by, trapped within, and lost by rampant, seductively truthful, but inevitably rogue coding. Architecture can resemble an aphorism we all interpret but cannot understand. Architecture can seem like an aphorism telling us we are all surrounded by emptiness. Drawings can open up the locked images of an architecture still to emerge. Gehry does that. Many architects do that. That these drawings are an emptiness filled with signs doesn't really help us. Or does it? Aphorisms usually hide such redesign behind the brevity of the form. The content is often as indeterminate and ambiguous as the form is closed and tight. Aphorisms, maxims about architecture and architects, are attractive because architecture cannot be held back by them. The very nature of an architectural haiku encourages an all-win, all-interpretation situation.

Aphorisms, like archobabble, are meaningless and full of meaning at the same time. That is why we can find the short haiku form used in periods of the strong Marxist-inspired days of the 1960s and 1970s passing over with the same dogma and passion to support phenomenology or the essence-inspired architectural poems of the 1980s and 1990s.[30] They account for architectural responsibility and moral stance but do little for the architecture itself. They comfort our opinions and interpretations, not our environments, as the Prince of Wales's contribution to architecture demonstrated. As we pointed out earlier, this particular vision of Britain was used in all good faith like an aphorism proclaiming only so much of what we love as God's country. And so much of what we don't love as a "monstrous carbuncle."[31]

Perhaps the "gap," like the architectural aphorism, like the drawing, helps reformulate architectural production and issue. Keeping haiku and Derrida in mind, architecture in the gap must always be a twofold process. First, it must seduce the reader into thinking it has something to say, something to communicate. That, in current architectural conditions, is dangerous enough. Second, having accepted the treachery of language, it must try to communicate this self-seduction. That is a double danger, because we have leapfrogged the reflexive dilemma. The public becomes fatigued with this type of dull honesty that exposes the very mechanics of failure. There is a third stage however, invited by the gap—the moment of natural, perpetual, and liberatory disruption.

In an architectural era that stutters to make any sense of itself, the commentator, historian, and critic risk becoming victims of the required reasoning needed to reestablish an order of sense. This is precisely the condition in architectural thinking and criticism today, shared by the bull and the useful aphorism that demands its own rules. As with a carnival that can operate only within a reinvention of its own significance, we suffer from the eagerness with which we want the solutions to be ours. We can then find ourselves lodged in suspended space. Our inner speech makes all sense out of external events, but this does not prevent us from misunderstanding just where we are coming from—stuck in a hopeless jargon, in a hopeless contemporary moment, inventing our own gap, inventing our own abyss between architecture and literature. Stuck—those students would say of me—somewhere between Ray Bradbury and William Gibson, in a fictional version of J. G. Ballard's novel *Crash*.

It is not impossible to see how Postmodernism offered a sort of pop cultural access to architectural symbol and metaphor, just as writers today see virtual reality offering the youth (and others) such access to information on the pop cultural data level. This naturally includes that access to information, if not experience, previously reserved for experts. To some, of course, it was and will remain the wrong access. But just as interfacing without engaging is a serious complaint only for those who cannot shift their own experience to fit circumstances advantageous and thrilling, so architecture might be seen to have been continually read by those in search of a formula with but a simplistic thesis to defend. It is certain that the shape-shifting, the juggling of cultural and critical tools, will still be able to deliver agendas before they are present in the architecture.

"Like computer hackers who understand the technology better than its adult users, the kids making drugs know more about the chemistry than the regulatory agencies." There is no doubt that Rushkoff's insight will be part of architecture's gap before we can say morphogenesis twice.[32] The gap, though, does not, will not, bring us any quicker to a reality resisted through architecture. Architectural truth might not only be doubly allergic to the gap; it might lie outside any language used about it. Which is precisely the bull we are speaking about.

What truth do we find in a drawing? Alvar Aalto, it is said, encouraged an architecture of doing, not talking. Considered tyrannical, autocratic, censoring an architectural discourse in the 1950s, Aalto's sketches, words, lectures, and interviews are now mined for the aphoristic gem. Aphoristically, a continual reinterpretation of Aalto's architecture looks likely to begin to stand in for a wishfulfilled progress in communication and meaning. But let us forget that the upset legacy of modern architecture and the modern code was long bypassed by language claims itself. Let us go to something more unusual. Anyone familiar with the writing of Roald Dahl will know that children respond fanatically to two things: laughter (humor) and any attack on the adults' way of doing things. There is architectural lesson here. A gentler version of this, but by no means less powerful, is Antoine St. Exupéry's story *The Little Prince*.[33] It is no accident that it begins with a drawing the narrator saw at age six of a boa constrictor.

Antoine St. Exupéry, drawings from *The Little Prince* (London: Pan Books, 1974). Reprinted by permission of Harcourt, Inc., and Editions Gallinard.

The narrator, somewhat like St. Exupéry himself, pondered deeply. He then succeeded, with the aid of a colored pencil, to complete his own drawing, "My Drawing Number One," the narrator said!

The narrator, age six, then proceeded to show his masterpiece to the grown-ups. What did they think? What did they see? Did it frighten them? Frighten them? Why should anyone be frightened by a hat? they said. Architectural lesson number one: ambiguity, repetition, and difference existed long before Roland Barthes, Julia Kristeva, Jacques Derrida, Gilles Deleuze, and poststructuralism. Indignant, disappointed, first-nail-in-the-coffin feeling, the narrator had to explain: "*My Drawing was not a picture of a hat. It was a picture of a boa constrictor digesting an elephant.*" But since the grown-ups were not able to understand it, the narrator decided to make another drawing. This was the drawing of the inside of a boa constrictor, so that the grown-ups could see it clearly. *"You see,"* the narrator said, *"they, grown-ups, always need to have things explained."* Architectural lesson number two: explanations, though redundant to the architectural experience, are always necessary. We know quite well what the grown-ups' response was: they still didn't know what the drawing was. This forced the narrator to give up a career as a magnificent artist and become a pilot. Architectural lesson number three: persevere, avoid explanations, and understand that adults, including architectural juries, committees, media hosts, universities, institutions, etc., don't understand anything by themselves.

The story unfolds. The narrator, like St. Exupéry, traveled all around the world, reluctant to show anyone his drawings anymore. Architectural lesson number four: keep drawing. Later, when the narrator meets the Little Prince on Asteroid B-612, he is asked to draw a sheep. Having given up drawing, the narrator took out, to show the Little Prince, one of the two pictures he had drawn so often: "'No, no, no!' the Little Prince replies. 'I do not want an elephant inside a boa constrictor. . . . What I need is a sheep. Draw me a sheep.'" This invited the narrator to make another drawing. Architectural lesson number five: Put the tongue away whenever necessary.

Where putting the tongue away has not quite been as important as it should, after Frank Lloyd Wright used to do it so brilliantly, we meet more and more world architects showing us the way. I refer here to architects like, amongst others, Herzog, Koolhaas, Eisenman, Jean Nouvel, and Gehry. It is not that they stop speaking; it is what they say and the way they say it. Nothing could be more appropriate to the contest in architecture, to the architectural bull, than putting the tongue away and still talking, still drawing.

To follow suit, it is worth attempting a summary of the poetics of the scribble and drawing as a point of departure for architecture. There is no doubt that architects will go on providing the drawings to fit their apparent gestalt raids, which is not, however, where myth originates. Drawings will always be able to perform the mystery they, if not the architecture, produce or then fail to express. But failure to express in architecture is different from the claims made for an architecture beyond language. In the more accessible language of *The Little Prince,* architecture has always hidden its secret in the depths of its heart. What gives architecture its beauty, like the house, the stars, and the desert, is something that is and remains invisible. With architecture so fluid, with the grown-ups wanting more and more explanations, seeing more and more the hat in the drawing, perhaps the only reasonable position in response to our mutual misunderstanding of each other is surely one of generosity: I might just know what you are trying to do.

We need only attend the fascination for chaos theory and its hijack by architecture to recall Russell on Hegel: "The worse your logic, the more interesting the consequences to which it gives rise." Architectural innocenti can move in theory, as if Richard Brautigan scripted *The Fish Thing* in architecture, but it is possible to use Frank Gehry's Guggenheim Museum in Bilbao as a metonym of other contemporary architecture, not for its form, nor for its "assured" or "dizzying" aesthetic endgame, but for its energy, its bull, its bardo and *fuerza* in architectural drawing, designing, and thinking. Bilbao offers a significance defined by Gehry's relentless way of reforming and recreating himself through his work. It is a reinvention of architecture through a persona that knows just when to put the tongue away, just when the drawing leaves off. This strategy is by no means as radical as it seems, for Gehry knows well enough that when the body stops fooling itself over differences, the realization of architecture begins. Knowing that one can abandon each scheme that appears unfolding from a sketch indicates an extraordinary controlled waywardness. It is an immense freedom, a type of essential redundancy (the paradox is perfect); it is the gap itself.

Surely, the lesson of such architecture is not in the metaphysics it does or doesn't bring to the architecture, nor the meaning that is or isn't there in its architecture. Instead, the lesson is in the unceasing itself, in the endless models, sketches, drawings, and studies. Architecture has become contest! The relentless method does not disguise the chaos; it parallels the obvious—architecture can emanate from the biscuit, a haiku, or crumpled paper. Whatever source culture privileges, whatever society turns into a consensus, architecture can make from it a liberating vision. And by repetition make from it an architectural mean, architectural consensus, and an ethical resonance. Jean Nouvel's connection to the moviemaker is pertinent: "When you're devoted to painting, writing or composing, you act alone, isolated from society, without any need for consensus. By contrast, a movie-maker or architect exists only through consensus."[34]

In the gap, Gehry shares with many contemporary architects today the astonishing ability to invent an architecture that comes in between today and tomorrow, that leases out control to other productive forces. From whatever source and with whatever traces already predisposed into architectural form (call it what you will, timing, production, and architecture) Gehry reinvents the Merzbau, the dada suicide in architecture. He also gives technology in the form of the Catia 3-D Modeller program a chance to revive architectural thrill. A smudge, a crumpled piece of paper, a doodle, a biscuit, haiku, a mathematical formula, chaos theory. Call it the serious architecture of frivolity if you like, call it rogue architecture or installation architecture. As the discourse shifts and New York entertains the continuing discourse of "lightness,"[35] it would be as well to remember, if St. Exupéry had not become a pilot and had become an architect instead, he would never have met the Little Prince. But then the Little Prince would probably have been written by Edmund Jabès: "Not knowing where you come from is almost tantamount to admitting that you come from nowhere. But that is silly. I held my tongue. I acted as if . . ." Jabès is taciturn. Having taken an essential distance from his own life, he contemplates whether his preference for silence did not grow out of always finding it difficult to feel he was from some place: "Even before I knew the desert, I knew it was my universe. Only sand can accompany a mute word all the way to the horizon. To write on sand, to listen to a voice from beyond time, all limits abolished."[36]

Jabès's desert, the white page, the blank sheet, the undrawn, all prompt us to return to the Little Prince in our interferences in architecture. During the course of his life the narrator, like the architect and the Jewish philosopher, like the Tibetan monk and the Little Prince, met many grown-ups. Even close up, the opinions of grown-ups never much improved. Whenever the narrator found one adult who might be clear-sighted, he would take out his Drawing Number One. It would be a test of true understanding. Do they really mind the gap? Do they really know when to leave language in the corridor? Do they really know when to let the breast emerge from the shoulder? Whoever it was, he, she, would always say upon looking at the drawing: That is a hat! The narrator then stopped talking of boa constrictors, stars, and forests. He would not speak of littoral areas where he could get his feet wet as the tide came in. Instead he would bring himself down to the level of the adult. He would talk about bridge, politics, and the books he had read. He would speak of philosophy and the way architectural theories were hijacking "sense." He would apply memetics to architecture and believe it a new theory. He wouldn't talk of the bull or the bardo. Instead he would compare neckties, scarves, phenomenology, and share prices. He would discuss deconstruction, the next discourse after "lightness," transmodernism, wine, and double-breasted suits. And the grown-up would be greatly pleased to have met such a sensible man!

₄ **archobabble** *on language and architecture*

The constant uncertainty may make everything seem bleak and almost hopeless; but if you look more deeply at it, you will see by that its very nature creates gaps, spaces in which profound chance and opportunities for transformation are continuously flowering—if, that is, they can be seen and seized.

—SOGYAL RINPOCHE[1]

Earlier we left Laurence Sterne describing the narrative of his novel, *Tristram Shandy,* as that line with a humpbacked *A,* a fire-burst *B,* some small events *c c c* and the even bigger humped, blowout *D* that punctured the narrative. From thereon the flourish of a huge "gap" opened up. Using Sterne's diagrams, it was possible to suggest general lines of critical interpretation and development by dividing twentieth-century architecture into the following two-score periods: futurism, 1900 to 1920; internationalism, 1920 to 1940; rationalistic modernism, 1940 to 1960; and plastic modernism 2, 1960 to 1980. How useful this remains is far from clear. Clearer is the fact that in the last twenty-year period of the twentieth century we were presented with a much more erratic, accelerated, exciting, and possibly self-canceling development in architecture.

Unremitting self-contradiction certainly has the terror and thrill of destabilizing the very privilege of the avant-garde, but does it have the potential for liberation, for transformation? It may be that a desire to fuse all, link all, and connect all is an architectural urgency we might never really become confident with. Indirectly hijacked by linguistics and philosophy, architectural terror was confiscated by linguistic promise. The sign of the sign and the floating signifier offered a pan-semiology in which literary studies institutionalized an architectural promise never previously achieved.[2] Fusing architecture with any discipline has left us more than ever residual, searching for escapable congruity and uncomfortable affinity.

In our investigation, we owe to Christopher Ricks and Sogyal Rinpoche what has been an understated and underlying development as we move on in our journey toward the final section, the possibility and potential of the architectural bull and bardo. Here it remains to hint at the bull as a resource, as something potential as much as something confusing: "the resource of a pressed, suppressed or oppressed people, a people on occasion pretending to be self-subordinated by foolishness so as the better to keep alive a secret self-respect and to be insubordinate and even safely 'provocative.'"[3]

For some thinking in contemporary architecture, safely provocative is now a virtual certainty and forces the question: if architecture is truly doomed by bad timing and ongoing claims for systems of truthful decoding, has it become too convenient to blame our own misundersanding of it? If the "bull" threatens each indiscretion with sarcasm and cynicism, a knowing wisdom more accessible than irony is suggested by the bardo. Language has hardly been innocent, but it will surely be a crime this century to be too safely provocative. Looked at this way, the twentieth century was lonely, our escape from it huge relief.

Such crossover urgency, interrelating architecture to incongruity and loaned images of thought might not only present architecture with a frivolity, a flippant flippancy, but with an unstoppable desire to undress architecture, as Georges Bataille might have put it, to the very impossible end. In this way we would be close to defining the architectural bardo as a critique of pure redundancy for architecture. This would be a bull beyond individual control, too safely provocative to be useful, too askew to rebuke wishfulness. If all this is to be ultimately bull, then we could interpret Laurence Sterne's last flourish rather differently. Is not all this discourse about confusion, unrest, and undoing architecture rather simpler than it looks? Is it not a gap dividing two sides? On one side we have an architecture seducing itself professionally with more and more apparently retrievable codes. Architecture in this case safely becomes a reading game in search for the stability of a symbolic order, a hysteria to hold back the last century to a promise of a "modern" architecture it now ought to attain. And on the other side, we have an architecture with a greater and more innovative nostalgia for the future. By necessity this is a thinking which unsteadies the conventions we try to bring to architecture. Perpetually swerving from it as historians, critics, and writers, this is an architecture that must go so close to self-cancelation as to announce, just as in language, *that it's all bull anyway!* A holding pattern, a consistent deferral, both approaches see the other sadly not as a gap but as an abyss. Is there no one out there crying, *"But things in architecture aren't that unsimple!"*[4]

In the last volume of *Tristram Shandy*, Sterne informs us that, in his narrative, he has scarce stepped out of his way.

Sterne means, in over three hundred pages, he has hardly deviated at all. "In fact, if I mend at this rate," Sterne continues, "it is not impossible—by the good leave of his grace of Benevento's devils—but I may arrive hereafter at the excellency of going on even thus:

---

which," Sterne says, "is a line drawn as straight as I could draw it, by a writing-master's ruler, (borrowed for that purpose) running neither to the left or to the right."[5] Sterne continues and provides yet another timely guide to the use of contradiction upsetting not itself, but all that we expect from its claims. Running neither to the right nor to the left, is this the architect's line? Is this the politician's line? The jury's line? The committee's line? The degree zero line for architecture? As we would expect from a clergyman, for the diagnosticians among us, Sterne delivers an architectural prognosis about this line:

This *right line,*—the path-way for Christians to walk in! say divines—
—The emblem of moral rectitude! says Cicero—
—The *best line,* say cabbage planters—is the shortest line, says Archimedes, which can be drawn from one given point to another—

The shortest line which can be drawn from one given point to another? Were the cabbage planters right? Did architecture make the mistake of looking for the shortest line to communicate what remain so often hazier, indistinct, mediocre, nomadic, seductive, acute, and contemporary? Was architecture so royally and easily duped in the twentieth century? And if so, what blame language?

In the fashion of undoing in architectural thinking, more is at stake than merely language. If we relinquish our hold on language, if we relinquish our conventional hold on architectural departure, source, production, and perception, we do not necessarily relinquish our hold on the entire shape of our lives and—in passing—an ethical response to architecture. It is not that unsimple. Though we live most of our lives in the shadow of architecture's reality, we also live in the essential redundancy of other disciplines to architecture. "The firing squad shoots in the back of the neck," the British dramatist Edward Bond wrote in a note to one of his plays. Whole nations may have been caught looking the wrong way! Whole disciplines, including architecture, may have been duped by language itself. "The greatest intellect is basically the most easily duped": Georges Bataille might have been speaking to us all. "To think that one apprehends the truth when one is only evading, vainly, the obvious stupidity of 'everyone.' "[6]

In Sterne's diagram it was the large blowout, or humped apparition marked *D*, that allowed us to appreciate how deconstruction punctured the narrative. Did it, or has it, as some believe, led architecture on the round, as the devils did in Sterne's novel? If language, more properly linguistics, attempted to make of architectural codes a legibility and pansemiology all its own, we must accept that it succeeded for a period, scaffolding architectural intention and meaning with a bullheaded, arrow-straight communication. Architecture had the advantage over literature of being able to avoid the retreat of the word itself. But at what cost?

The twentieth century saw architecture fail against its own silent articulation, failing also to recognize its own bull. In writing architecture we might ask, why, did we forget Socrates?

The fact is, Phaedrus, that writing involves a similar disadvantage to painting. The productions of painting look like living beings, but if you ask them a question why, they maintain a solemn silence. The same holds true of written words; you might suppose that they understand what they are saying, but if you ask them what they mean by anything they simply return the same answer over and over again. Besides, once a thing is committed to writing it circulates equally among those who understand the subject and those who have no business with it; a writing cannot distinguish between suitable and unsuitable readers. And if it is ill-treated or unfairly abused it always needs its parent to come to its rescue; it is quite incapable of defending or helping itself.[7]

Though there have been attempts to avoid the crutches of linguistics and semantics by a deception and seduction of brevity, much architecture at the end of the twentieth century remained trapped in a latent exercise in the architectural semiotic. Semantics and ambiguity did give way to the architectural poem, but it was one that begged another truthfulness to emerge out of even more decoding. Buildings were disguised as lectures, poems that were emotive, self-fulfilling, metaphoric laments. Shifting dogma from Karl Marx to Maurice Merleau-Ponty, the legacy was wish fulfilment, hoping against hope that the suitable truth reaches the suitable readers who are found for the suitable architecture.

A semantic approach to architecture, however—architecture as a legible, readable, decodable, and hence an oversimplified communicating act—was actually embedded deep in the modern code. Already, as early as the Moscow and Prague linguists of the 1930s, as early as Viktor Schklovsky's *defamiliarization* and Lev Vygotsky's insights into inner speech, warnings against oversimplifying communication and agitprop models were made. They were not readily heeded. Siegfried Giedion mostly ignored linguistic research, opting for straight-arrow architectural comment and ideology. Current research is only now indicating how this was orchestrated to conform to the masonic club of international architecture. Much later, Charles Jencks's thesis, published in 1973 as *Modern Movements in Architecture,* ensured that an open structuralism emphasized the critical "reading" act for architecture. The result, however, was more dramatic.

Architecture as a reading exercise anticipated a cat-and-mouse game. Critics with their interpretative acts, historians with their critical acts, exchanged places with the architect. Prescriptions ruled as it became musical chairs time! For the next twenty years after 1973, architects played this cat-and-mouse game with a supposed legibility and public access in architectural coding. Genres of architecture were subjected to reading exercises, encouraging architects to be recognized by their stylistic moves and "signatures." Clearly, it encouraged, too, an architectural market.

The drama in this architectural market was in the detachment between the language used and the buildings achieved. Reversals were made where architects imagined the success of the messages and the building's communication before the eventual architecture was built. Commissions were often awarded on critical claims, leaving the realized architecture to go through scenarios of disappointment and ideological rebuttals. At times it was a thrilling if stupid period, but a "certain wisdom" should have warned us. "Stupidity," Milan Kundera has it, "does not give way to science, modernity, progress; on the contrary, it progresses right along with progress."[8] Has this stupidity progressed right along with architectural progress?

Is it as Sisyphean as Solà-Morales describes when he assesses this "hopeless" critical condition inherent in any topography? "The task of criticism is a labour of Sisyphus. Every effort at capturing the aesthetic potential of the artwork is condemned to ultimate sterility."[9] This, the bardo meeting the bull again, is why reality will always be more potent than thought, but why the passion within the paradox keeps us throwing words into the architectural abyss.

The ideological rebuttals flattened out as the "Age of Discourse" took over, an age in which many hitchhiked attractive ideas and other disciplines for architectural reward. Raiding the French thinkers was more than architectural hip, it was the coolest thing around besides hovering for a Perrier in the "Hotel Architecture" lounge bar. "Philosophy was hijacked and after more architectural fidgetting," as Frank Heron writes, "architects became competent leap-froggers of knowledge."[10] Jencks considered this a change from the Age of the Proletariat to the Age of the Cognitariat. It was, however, only a change in seduction. According to Jencks's incredibly seductive, one-man literary critical show, architects not only recognized the boa constrictor eating the elephant in the Little Prince's drawing. Now architects could produce schemes that would narrate what the snake had for breakfast, and buildings that could tell about the metaphysics of the elephant. Architects confronted the gap, tempted the void, and pulled at the abyss in order to learn to tease out meaning even if it was not present in architecture. The cleverness and sophistry extended to unimaginable rogue strategies for the urban jungle. Now, in the new millennium, with all this "joke knowledge" strapped to the architectural body like oxygen tanks, architecture has entered the fourth stage, the Age of Discourse: it is surfing.[11] Surfing, that is, with an architectural knowledge so lightly gained, so thinly masked, so keenly contested, so dazzlingly loaned, so aggressively resisted, but of which so much is expected. Surfing with Hegel, Husserl, and Heidegger inevitably gave over to a newer team; no longer Derrida and Deleuze but Maurice Blanchot and Virilio, or Jabès and Emmanuel Levinas.[12] Is it now so lonely in architecture that takes us to the edge of our own knowledge? Louis Althusser knew the danger of the bull, the *canular*. Cancel out the self often enough and all else goes![13]

Even if architecture is not that unsimple, it looks as if it will need this self-canceling stage more than ever in this new century. Protection is in the provocation. Attempt to avoid the language of the "court" discourse, and one is accused of a wilful, irresponsible individualism. Architectural writing, the use it has made of language, chases a world of private meaning always with the danger that it runs into the production of architecture itself. Only now are we beginning to see the results from endless attempts to "construct the word." What has changed? Did not Karl Kraus say of the Loos House in Vienna, "That's not a house he has built, but a thought?"

After the influence of deconstruction (the Heideggerization of architecture in and through Jacques Derrida?) we cannot take for granted that the life-world constructs that architecture should connect with are amputated. Nor can we assume that architecture is doomed to follow fiction and the fallen form of language in a celebration of the redundancy and pornography of gratuitous metaphysics in architecture. There does, however, seem to be a battle on. To some, an architecture finally jettisoning the "modern code" and fulfilling a permanent ephemeral promise takes us further and further away from any professional identity and the demands for a social, ethical, and political responsibility for architecture. To others, the architectural visions approaching philosophical limit are not so much philosophies of inaction as interaction. Looked at anew, the challenge for investigation is to find in these architectures an identity and collective responsibility forming even from improbable personal architectures. It is also a challenge to determine whether this autonomous shudder, the privatization of architects into Duchamps-to-themselves, has more than unscience and disengagement to offer, whether influenced by poststructuralism or a cyberspace menu!

For those seeking to go beyond disengagement, beyond architecture's current deradicalization, these architectural encounters are important alibis for grander spatial and political encounters. If this is an unnecessary and unstoppable dualism in architecture (the social mission versus disengagement) we have seen how other disciplines continue to add further unrest. For both camps, however, it begins to look like stalemate time, unless we can unravel some of the false good ideas language, linguistics, and writing about architecture have recently given us. If architecture fails to disengage itself from the seduction of form and image, theory and the constructed word will continue as an autonomous, redundant exercise into the anxiety of language first, with architecture itself always running a weak second. Peter Eisenman has been wrongly held responsible for the frivolous use of the weakness of the architectural sign. Usually the skill at missing the point of such discourse passes to lesser talents, but we need be warned: "Architecture is a very weak condition of sign—sign in the sense of dealing with absences. Metaphorically, architecture is notoriously weak." [14]

And "weak" is language itself in relation to this weakness. Architecture is ahead of language, inviting offers it cannot refuse, drawings invested with more meaning than is possible, photographs it swoons at, critical scheming it feels comfortable with. Of course, such arguments about language's weakness play into the hands of those who claim that the frivolity of the last century is traceable to the very romance of Saussure and the use and abuse of linguistics and the arbitrary sign. This may be the false good idea that the twentieth century is paying for as it tried to identify those visual systems that can be subsumed under language systems without residue. Thankfully, this century can allow us to live more residually than ever.

Many architects feel lucky. Unseduced by language concerns, uninterested in the constructed word, ignorant of the way movements worked this century meant that passing attention only was given to such theoretical flirtations. Architects with little knowledge of language's "promise" applauded themselves for that fortunate ignorance while hijacking the loaned images and metaphors of philosophy for a particular form of souvenir architecture. Risking conclusions before the research, philosophical undoing has now became the alibi for everything wrong in architecture. This has reinforced the failure of architecture's promise to the public who, invited so rarely into the serious debate about the constructed word, have inevitably sided on the spectacular, the rise and rise of the architectural image.

It has also been fashionable to dump the discourse. In collective ignorance, serious complaints gained ground. The "discourse" centers of New York and Tokyo were felt suspect; discourse itself became suspect and loose. Yet as Martin Jay reminds us, despite these contrary and shifting usages, despite professional betrayal by architectural language, "discourse remains the best term to denote the level on which the object of this enquiry is located, that being a corpus of more or less loosely interwoven arguments, metaphors, assertions, and prejudices that cohere more associatively than logically in any strict sense of the term."[15]

Suspicious about discourse, the idea of a "built thought" has been deradicalized by professional lament at theory, philosophy, and language invading architecture. Returning to Sterne's little humped blowout, what can we make of these attempts at the constructed word? Are we faced with an abyss of unmeaning and undoing, an architecture condemned to the anxiety of the language we can use about it, that is, an architecture permanently askew symbolizing the "literal" unsettling avant-garde, a critique then of its own pure redundancy? It is, of course, possible to imagine some gain from the anxiety and unrest architecture faces with the language used about it. The ultimate effect of philosophical contest in architecture is the disruption of the guardians of a cultural tradition.

The ultimate effect of philosophical contest? The bull is always on good terms with writing architecture askew. There is and can be no ultimate effect of philosophical contest. In architecture, in cuisine, tragic might be all this instability, but the disruption of convention surely is not tragic. Claims that this "undoing" is the death of architecture as we know it are misplaced. If we want some encouragement for this confusion, Ricks is a better guide than Sam Shepard. Architecture might not be "abstracted to death" by all this undoing, but it might be an abstract of death itself. This might be akin to the painful bardo of dying, "which lasts from the process of dying right up until the end of what is known as the 'inner respiration.'" We are reminded of Hejduk's pathognomy introduced at the beginning of these essays. The bewildering relativity of this carnival stage in architecture will be pulled back by imagination itself, by what the Tibetans speak of as a "ground luminosity."[16] It is a rebirth, and needs to be, for, as Hejduk says, with death there is no pulling back. If it makes sense to reverse all this upset, we might also relocate ourselves happily in the bull. With death there is no architecture unless we pull back.

Of course all the "undoing" in architecture can also be interpreted as theories to construct the rope ladder across the ravine and lead us toward an architecture against architecture itself. If there is an architecture of such lightness and frivolity, an architecture of the fireworks display, then it is an architecture similar to poetry in all things but one—realization. Georges Bataille also recognized the alibi poetry could be for our own contemporary moment: "Poetry was simply a detour:

through it I escaped the world of discourse, which had become the natural world for me." [17] Architecture has always played off poetry. "With poetry," Bataille continues, "I entered a kind of grave where the infinity of the possible was born from the death of the logical world."

Apart from those seriously twisting architecture's arm with philosophical rigor and doubt, deconstruction allowed architects to escape the very discourse they thought they entered, while it allowed theorists to claim for architecture the space philosophy never ultimately achieves. The rebound of architectural coding from the critic back to the architect ultimately offered a predictability where architects stylistically altered signatures through a weak strategy of difference and repetition. Glance at the stringent and inaccessible "archobabble" made from such thinkers passing for architectural philosophy and theory, and one cannot be in much doubt about the kind of grave that language has been preparing for an architecture born from the death of the logical world.

Possibly the bardo in Deleuze, not Derrida, offers us a way out. Can architecture, like words, go dead on us? Some take this dislocation of meaning as a mistaken turn in architecture, as philosophical flirtation, a mediated activity reasserting language as a foil to ideas of progress. We are reminded of Leach's Euler diagram; falling short of fetishization seems to be the acceptable limit of such activity. To undo thought through philosophy may be one thing. To see it undo architecture is quite another. It now looks possible that "undoing" may have architects missing the point of their own talent. Or then it is merely the bull that has been missed, as philosophy begins to trickle down to more than a generation and the language used and abused within architecture creates so many generalizations about architectural promise that it is difficult to come back to Earth. Is this the zero-degree cyber point: cold earth, bitch of a planet. No return!

Is it true that this attraction to the "death of the logical world"—this undoing—has not only upset architectural thinking but rendered architecture untouchable by the demands and concerns of contemporary life? It is not. As we offer our knowledge to thinness, and the thinness of language invites more and more distrust the more we are challenged. Is this a sustainable plea? Such a thinness does not necessarily imply a thinness of architecture; there is such a thing as intensive weakness, lost in careful privacy until it finds the expressible. This is the invisible, the alibis that, against the odds, produce an unimaginable architecture in the new millennium. In the wrong hands, of course, these are hardly attractive errors.

Architecture carried out under the disguises of death and unrest, chaos and indeterminacy, under oscillating conditions is no less contemporary than an architecture of more apparent visual and symbolic transfer. Those who resist this upset and undoing might be right in trying to restore a grounding in a normative grammar for an architecture of symbolic transfer. This is a way of making sense from the uncertainty, a sense considered to suit a necessary "symbolic and social order" for architecture. Though this still relies on the architectural semiotic, it might be seen as a preparation for social change. But can it alter the mechanics by which change is brought about?

"Not to settle for, not to be unsettled by. "[18] The "gap" can never be final. Architecture thought out or thought through in a confusing time need not be an expression of that confusion. Unless we explore the profession's own history of "reading" architecture, unless we unmake some of the critical truths that have predisposed a future, architecture will be at the mercy of those schemes that claim an irretrievable impoverishment in experiencing architecture. Unless we explore the vocabulary and jargon allowed for the informed cultural audience, unless we consider whether it is language or architecture that constitutes today's architectural hoodwink, we will also get no further than the partisan debate.

Today, there is a fever in architecture for the tolerable straight line. It has become fashionable to denigrate this "undoing" in architecture and see a return to silence, to eternal values. This deradicalism, however, misses the point of the energy of change and unrest around in contemporary architecture. Such easy denigration flattens out too quickly, reducing all unwanted architecture to an untalented range of postmodern or poststructural stances. This denigration also sees architecture as a compromized professional practice using "illegibility" as a tool for personal meaning. It also misses the point of current research, for it is "legibility" in culture that has long been unsteady by being subservient to the same dynamics that propel fashion and advertising. Unless we trace the way visions and codes have preoccupied a more general audience with promises of a meaningful (fashionable? truthful?) architecture, we will probably get no nearer to understanding why contemporary architecture is considered unconnected to the community and culture's memory. We will get no further than Brodsky's desire to cuckhold the architect for doing what the bomber and terrorist failed to do. We will also get no further than Sunday-supplement rudeness toward architects.

When much of the new architecture attempts communication beyond a reduction to language we stumble. When someone like Jean Nouvel attempts to collide his architecture with the locality's need for memorable images, where does the energy fall short? In cinema? Can we still continue to deny that architecture is one supplier of memorable and memetic images? Double coding was always a limited gamble for the ambiguity forever present in architecture. What, then, are the consequences for the meaning of architectural experience becoming ultimately our own, ecstatic but unsharable?

Provocative and thrilling, restless and uncertain, contemporary architecture conforms to a more serious identity for architecture. It is often an aggressive and confrontational rebuttal to flat historicist legacies and political shortcomings. In this way the architecture it seeks, the dislocation of meaning it invites, the holding pattern it occupies, are necessarily as autonomous and as entrepreneurial as ever. We can now see how the Johnsons of the world in the 1980s organized the carnival. Only some, very few, orchestrated it. And if the carnival gained strength, it is obvious that juxtaposition and displacement, dagger or shard, computer fidgetry and architectural morphing shared the same aesthetics with advertising, journalism, fashion, and literature. One does not necessarily demote the activity of the other, as an aid to, say, the tectonics and typology necessary to the architectural exercise. Meanwhile, a fake historicism has turned cities into indiscriminate theme parks where street scene reconstruction becomes heritage art. Debates on "bigness" take over from societies that have nothing but bigness to offer! The really brave architect might already be turning all this into theater before the computer screens do it for us. But it is too late! Even turbulence has been legitimized as yet another metaphor, another stylistic trope, of architectural infinity. Chaos science or fractal theory become instant alibis, superstructural aid to the conceptual (tectonic, topographic, and typological) logic from which buildings and architecture must attempt to communicate.[19] Is this the fashionable bull-end of architecture's undoing?

Until architecture begins understanding the lost logic by which it wants, yet might fail to communicate as symbol, as space, as type, it remains seriously adrift. And yet how can we speak of architecture seriously adrift and not coincide it with our contemporary moment? How can we use phrases like "until architecture begins understanding the lost logic" if the very rigor of thinking askew produces an architecturally askewed logic? Architecture, after all, only exists through what is made of it, through what is realized and rejected from its language scaffold. Made up as a discourse, however silent, however allergic to the language used about it, architecture must always be more than the cabbage planter's straight line. Reality is always more pertinent, otherwise it is a series of buildings, built forms, spaces to which we apply a system and critical scheme in order to convince ourselves of its functional and social purposes, which has nothing to do with the shared task that architecture has taken on itself. Should it be forbidden to ask anymore just what is the social construction of architecture's reality beyond the construction of a fashionable and inventive non-sense?

To take language and architecture seriously, would we not need to have an idea of how jargons of authenticity become authentic jargons, how discourse rules as long as it remains recognizable? Perhaps we can take a more unusual way of doing this by turning to one of Rudyard Kipling's *Just So Stories* from 1902, "How the Alphabet Was Made." Taffy, a young neolithic girl, asks her father Tegumai to make a noise, any noise. Tegumai says, "Ah! Will that do?" Taffy thinks this noise made by her father looks like a carp's mouth. She takes the birch bark, and on it she draws what she sees by scratching with a shark's tooth. Tegumai asks Taffy why she would need this. Taffy wants it as a sign that will remind her father of the "ah" noise. She could then use it to remind him of surprise. Taffy attempts to draw the carp but finds that she can only draw something that means a carp's mouth. She settles for a drawing of the mouth, which she says means "Ah!" Tegumai finds this reasonable but tells his daughter that she has forgotten the feeler that hangs across the fish's mouth. Taffy complains: she can't draw. Tegumai assures her that she need draw only the opening of the mouth with the feeler across. Taffy proceeds to copy this drawing and asks her father if he would understand it if she drew this. "Perfectly," Tegumai said when he saw the third drawing. "And I'll be quite as s'prised when I see it anywhere as if you had jumped out from behind a tree and said, 'Ah!' The exclaimed "Ah" of architecture's jargon reminds us of the same thing. "Ah," we might say, the jargon

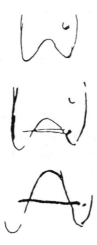

How the Alphabet Was Made, drawings from Rudyard Kipling, *Just So Stories* (New York: Penguin Popular Classics, 1994), pp. 94–95. Reprinted by permission of A. P. Watt Ltd. on behalf of The National Trust for Places of Historic Interest or Natural Beauty.

of architecture is no longer authentic, it has leapfrogged the very sources and disciplines it came from. "Ah," how then do we find whether some discourses are more authentic than others? Are not some jargons more architecturally correct than others? Let us recall Witold Gombrowicz:

All the mechanisms of an increasingly mechanized culture which have led art to become increasingly artificial, the poet to become more of a "poet," the painter more of a "painter," the genius more of a "genius," rose in value and such an overdone, elaborate language has imposed itself that today, in Paris, people no longer really know what they are saying."[20]

Jargon predisposes us to navigate and resist, but to do so skillfully if we want to participate in architecture's discourse. In his *Modern English Usage* (1926), H. W. Fowler has this to say on Jargon:

Jargon is talk that is considered both ugly-sounding and hard to understand: applied especially to; (1) the sectional vocabulary of a science, art, class, sect, trade, or profession, full of technical terms (cf. Cant, slang); (2) hybrid speech of different languages; (3) the use of long words, circumlocution, and other clumsiness.[21]

And other clumsiness? How can we attend to a time when jargon was authentic, and when might that have been during the last century? Was there even a time in the golden days of modern architecture when the firing squad didn't shoot in the back of the neck? We might ruffle the feathers of jargon a little if we return to Sterne's hump-bubble, which we characterized as deconstruction.

Have deconstruction and other constructed words really suggested an undoing of architecture out to jettison its social mission in favor of the disengaged, postradical space? Or can we attend more to Venturi's doubt as well as his writing in his iconography and electronics?

Those of us who respect and love the Modern architecture of sixty years ago and have learnt immeasurably from it are offended by the Neo-Modern parody of it. Yet perhaps we should not be. Decon, whose decorative use of structural elements is the ultimate "construction of decoration," may be today's equivalent of Art Deco—that poignant and beautiful last attempt by the rear guard to graft the old

Beaux-Arts on to the new International Style. Perhaps Art Decon is the Art Deco of POMO. That ironical last gasp was effective and had its place. Is the Decon we are flailing a dying, but not dead, horse?"²²

What does language aid, in all its fissures, disruption, and dissolution, and what does writing and jargon indicate for an architecture beyond more and more constructed words? That inner respiration or that last gasp? As redundant alibis for constructing culture's own logic, ideas represented by jargon are no more fallible than metaphors of nature and culture, of art and technology. Where and how are we to return, if indeed we should, through such language and jargon to the evidence, to the ethics and experience of the buildings themselves?

The fragility of architecture and its responsibility concerns each one of us. The "normative" lectures on what architecture should be doing, what architecture is not doing, what architecture will never do, continue to encourage us to bypass the normative, where it tells us how to live, how to dwell, how to feel, how to narrativize, how to philosophize, and how to prey to the higher gods. Getting nowhere fast, such a "bull" asks us to leave aside an architecture when it plays a hypnotic trick on itself, when it offers architecture as psychotherapy for the architects' own incompatibility with the contemporary moment, or when it offers an architecture of nostalgia for historical sign and plays the Johnny Mnemonic game.

"Minding the gap" is neither resistance in architecture nor rehabilitation. It is to see architecture fluid, fragile to its own bardo thinking, responsible to its own realization, open to its own bull, becoming its own critique of redundancy. Certainly an architecture open to the discourses beyond its discipline, but beyond Vitruvius, Alberti, Aristotle? There are indications that the assault on meaning and language will tire us. Signs are that the fragmentation of self will also tire us as the marginal and anxious border states may prove too difficult to inhabit. But not without effect.

Rod Mengham uses the term the "human muddle" to describe a direction in language. There are now signs that this human muddle, rather than the "originary ideal of language," will be viewed as a creative force in architecture. And muddle over idealism need not necessarily mean more voodoo, more archobabble. The Tibetans see it in entirely another way. Let us be quite clear. Any number of architectures are capable of jargons of authenticity. Any architectures, whatever doctrine or style, story or thesis, can benefit from operational and critical myths. Whether other disciplines are useful as operative myths for architectural contest remains open, but however rampant these myths, some are clearly more attractive than others. Some, too, like film and linguistics, are more accessible than others and—possibly—more fallacious than others. Any building, too, can unsettle any chosen architectural vocabulary as fast as it could claim to unsettle the iconography of the vertical or the horizontal. Any building can resemble Godzilla, grade B movies, a car crash, or grade B thinking. Any building, serial event of architecture can even simulate "the authenticity of being." Any architecture with a little geo-tectonic fudging can be considered as far or as near to nature as required. All it requires is more cultural fidgetting of the sort we have gotten used to. Coding—double coding, triple coding, multicoding, transcoding, etc.—might have done little more than recode architecture's self-importance.

More language, more voodoo, more babble? The desire to hold back some architecture to an architectural significance through language will obviously conform to whichever group orchestrates this significance, as we said earlier. We must continually warn ourselves. In an unstable age, instability is never as radical as it seems. There is a seductive safety, even a deradicalism, in provocation. Like casualness and lightness, provocation needs untapped rigor and discipline in its use and abuse of both language and architecture.

It is no coincidence that the problematization of meaning needs the "sign" as much as it needs to sign off. If this is a thrilling stage at which architecture jettisons the modern code reliance on a simplistic sign-signifier relationship and fulfills a permanent ephemeral promise, then it begs to be helped by other disciplines.[23] As we saw with architecture aided and prompted by film as a discipline, we are again invited into those as yet untheorized and even untenable architectures of a privatized sort. Who knows whether this takes us nearer those personal architectures chosen from a cyberspace menu? But could we hazard a guess that we might be entertaining an architecture gone beyond the anxiety of language and into the very real upset of the image? An upset that probably involves an oscillation in a way hithertoo unseen in architectural experience so far?

Within all the talk, within the archobabble, we already recognized one solid strategy of putting the tongue away. Architects, some more than others, can talk a good game. Some have the Althusser skill of using language to support the architectural a priori and scaffold architectural purpose. In between the noise, the babble of seminar and studio, and in between political resistance, real issues of our contemporary life are smuggled through. Some of these issues reach architecture— at present hardly enough. But it can happen. So restless, so poetic, so much in error with itself, we might say that architecture today has never had it so good—a paradox no longer out of reach.

The very fragility of our redundant condition is crucial. Whatever authenticity we give to the jargon used about architecture, today's dualism, today's dissatisfaction, and carnival maneuvers in the conference circuit represent a grand emptying out and also an architecture to come—architecture having no head! This emptying decapitation is a condition undressing each and every one of us. Architecture cannot fall back on tried schemes, known styles, and systematic replundering. It must engage the "gap," return to fragility and responsibility, as each of us is to blame for what we cannot blame in architecture. Recognizing this, we will serve the new century better by mining our own errors in the last. We could rehearse for an architecture to come by understanding what frauds were played on us in the last century. This complements the grand nostalgia for a future unknown, not a redefined past.

As we have discussed in these essays, architecture can hijack other disciplines, literature, dance, poststructuralism, cuisine, boxing, t'ai chi, and psychoanalysis. Architecture can leapfrog areas of knowledge that it may not need or understand—or which do not conform to the pictures we require. Architecture can go on and do this with any amount of dazzling applications until it ends up surfing, say, with Max Weber or Kierkegaard, not with Deleuze or Virilio. Architecture can try to be even

cleverer in its own blindness. It could also extend its own redundancy to a critical "mood" or "mode" within its own production. It could do this simply by leaving the computer open,
extending this impossible idea to architecture as an event of
violence, of discourse, of politics, of social, not individual,
production.

In its discourse we can say everything and anything about
architecture. Architecture would be on a roll, and we would
be enjoying ourselves. Jean Baudrillard closes in on such redundancy, on the bull waiting up there in front for us: "If
things exist, there is no use believing in them. If they do not
exist, there is no use renouncing them."[24] Architecture then
becomes what it has always been, the bardo—a passage from
one life to another. Paul Auster writes:

"Sleep was a passage from one life into another, a small death in
which the demons inside him had caught fire again, melting back
into the flames they were born of. It wasn't that they were gone, but
they had no shape anymore, and in their formless ubiquity they had
spread themselves through his entire body—invisible yet present, a
part of him now in the same way that his blood and chromosomes
were, a fire awash in the very fluids that kept him alive. He did not
feel that he was any better or worse than he had been before, but he
was no longer frightened. This was the crucial difference. He had
rushed into the burning house and pulled himself out of the flames,
and now that he had done it, the thought of doing it again no longer
frightened him."[25]

Reading Auster reminds us of Hejduk's warnings so early
on in this book, but with a crucial difference. The thought of

doing it again should now no longer frighten architecture. Yet we are pulled back. Something tugs at our sleeves. Perhaps the cabbage planters or other devils. They force us to acknowledge, while we are enjoying all this talk, that the very rigor of the language that we want to invest into architecture needs this redundant condition. Reality is somewhere else. Then we come down to Earth slowly like the Little Prince, who was not able to stand up again: "There now, that is all."

But he hesitated. Then the Little Prince got up: "There was nothing there but a flash of yellow close to his ankle. He remained motionless for an instant. He did not cry out. He fell as gently as a tree falls. There was not even any sound, because of the sand."[26]

The snake. There was zero but it was not nothing.

Is it so easy to speak and write about architecture as a fiction of a world we only want to read about? Edmond Jabès or Antoine de St. Exupéry? "Being partisan or an opponent to a particular work is, a-priori, suspect."[27] Architecture needs this zero, it needs the bull, it needs the bardo, to know what value and purpose remains. We, too, need the redundancy to know how fragile, how responsible we are and architecture is. We need the bull, long in use before being associated only with the Irish and language: "a self-contradictory proposition; in modern use, an expression containing manifest contradictions in terms or involving a ludicrous inconsistency unperceived by the speaker."[28]

Today the polish remains in some buildings, the angles tilt, the slabettes arch less in agony and overlay, the integers are unsteady, glass and fabric-stretch is everywhere, transparency is achieved, as is fraudulence and instability, and the sensuality

of rocked planes keep crashing through the interiors like a spit-
fire entering the lonely restaurant of contemporary architecture. Architecture is finally undone by language. Long live
architecture! To which we must put the loveliest and saddest
landscape in the world, from St. Exupéry next to Jabès's desert.
Sand!

5 seize the bull *toward the bull and bardo*

The bull is busy sawing off the branch we and it are sitting
on. A risky comic turn, and one which is creepily factitious
when down below there are flunkeys with cushions to break
your fall.

—CHRISTOPHER RICKS[1]

A stage in life is reached where our positions and our age de-
mand from us what we might call "a certain wisdom." Unrest
or uncertainty in ideas, even in life itself, is generally supposed
to disappear. We are, for all intents and purposes, expected to
offer models, ideas, and proposals that appear mature. We are
expected to speak in complete sentences even if we have difficulty uttering them. And despite confessing this difficulty, we
must still stand by them. If we vomit before speaking we are
supposed to be beyond that infantile stage. Even if we cannot
stabilize our "body of knowledge" or keep to one or other
purifying episteme it is still considered time to come home.
Do we forget the slogans, the haikus, and the aphorisms? To
be "comfortably numb" is a luxury we can no longer afford.
Yet indifference can remain with us for so long that it becomes
essential to define its passion.

Without a belief that buildings can be "read," that which
invites architecture to engage us in a higher level of organiza-
tion would lose its alibi. Without a belief that architecture can
be decoded and recoded, architecture cannot characteristically
represent unfolding, cultural, and social processes. Nor without these hopes can architecture signify changing and growing

structures that reflect our contemporary moment more than others. Architecture as a literal or abstract symbol of theories of convergence, emergence, chaos science, cosmogenesis, or any other such displaced metaphorical agony, assumes that we are still trying to read architecture "correctly," despite years of being told that nothing, not even architecture, is done straight anymore. Without this fragile system of beliefs, it is likely that there may be no new languages of architecture at all—no post-modern, no deconstruction, no new-modern, no romantic-modern, no transmodern—merely new moves in an old game.[2] To run with this logic, it cannot surely be long before redundancy theory offers itself as the higher level of organiza-tion for architecture, thereby legitimating a self-correcting, self-canceling, transparent layering of all architecture's prom-ise. Is this the architectural bull?

Some architects have the confidence of a Bogart or a Beck-ett, not a Baudrillard or a Blanchot. Frank Gehry, for example, speaks as if scripted by Kurt Schwitters. At a symposium on "Art and Technology" at the Zitelle Foundation during the 1995 Venice Biennale, both Allen Ginsberg and Frank Gehry were together on a panel of illuminati.[3] After two hours of continuous personalizing statements on the theme, after Gins-berg's seductive gnostic mantras punctuated by the Italian translator and ecstatic applause, like the narrator in the Little Prince, do we not do our best to remember the grown-up's words? Just what did they say? Just what did they mean? Is it just by chance that Gehry's words come to mind, seem easier to recall? Are they simpler, repetitive, memetic, or aphoristic? Or demotic? Or all these?

Gehry, however, not as natural a raconteur as Frank Lloyd Wright, knows just when to hang words in the breeze, when to leave language lying about in the corridor. As an architect, he knows when to allow a drawing to speak for more than it can, perform for more architecture than is present. Others, like Jean Nouvel, also let provocation describe the epoch as much as their architecture while achieving remarkably different results. Because our era takes its misfortunes seriously, speaking, performing, and conferencing have become part of the epoch. As movement and in movement, these activities communicate the contemporary moment as much as architecture but are never as real, never quite as vulnerable. Language can always be left lying in the corridor or walked past along with the empty Coke cans, yesterday's paper, and old opera tickets. Is there not a serious point here?

Leaving language lying in the corridor is one reason why some architects infuriate other professionals. Some, like Gehry, appear to be listening to everyone else speaking, as if it were only others who represent "a certain wisdom" and they are just making up the team. Not surprising to overhear: "Frank Gehry is inventing the only way possible to be absolute and American at the same time." What could it possibly mean to speak of architecture from an architect as absolutely American in an American place? Is this a cinematic definition where the image is already the moving subject of architecture? Or is it a photographic definition where the surface becomes an irremedial facade? Are Gehry and Rauschenberg's binoculars in Los Angeles the upturned result of sculpture freed from a toothpaste image of softness? Just what have these installations got to do with architecture's own programs?

Let us reflect a last time on the interferences played out by
film on architecture: film offering architecture alibis, film as a
quotidian reference system for architectural sign, film as structure and/or approach in the architectural process, and film as
a series of dazzling images for metaphoric heist. Concepts of
rapid succession, radical montage, dynamic processes, and the
increase in image-making software see theoretical architecture
commit itself to extending the theories of film and digitalization. Software becomes the impulse and montage for residual
space in urban configurations with digital residue. Digitalization takes over cinema as its own edge project for architecture.
"Screen" once more responds to and redefines architectural
"scene."

Combine these contemporary impulses to shape architecture's new mission and we begin to see them as more than
providers of theoretical and stylistic props, motives, and
morphs for new representations in architecture. Yet the reality
is somewhat flatter. Perceptions of urban and rural environments become less sequences of ruptured architectural convention and resemble more installatory and scenographic hoaxes,
the failed, thinner end of replication as it once more answers
too hastily the call for legibility in architecture. Would it be
unfair to think that film and architecture were paired together
because of a crisis in architectural criticism? And what of digitalization now? The legacy of cultural and architectural relativism over the last three decades has proved devastating. So
private are our worlds, critical practice struggles, as it must, to
create any shared ground. Suffering, criticism then begins to
carnivalize itself, repeating and replicating tired schemata.[4]
And when such free-for-all occurs, criticism so often seeks

more than mere support from other disciplines. Some argue that such support does little more than predetermine weak architectures of filmic and digitalized importance. Refiguring architecture with fresh source, this delays the closure of the modernist project by using film as a belated serial event. New, innovative computer software allowing seamless projected curves suggest that architecture will use new materials and opt for a holding pattern, even less arrival than was ever imagined possible.

Frank Gehry speaks, perhaps misleadingly, of a scary world. He speaks of a son who thinks his might be the Last Generation. He speaks of art and technology as having seventy computers, none of which he can switch on. But when switched on, of course, the programs transform the drawing or the scribble into a series of sophisticated planes, interactive forms, and an architectural modeling previously handled by the modern movement's own architectural origami. Will only intuition and the "deep structures of the psyche" arrest this digital runaway? As in a Gehry drawing, the context within digitalization is often hard to make out.

Gehry talks of the "fish thing" just as Aalto, a great raconteur, spoke epigrammatically and mischievously of the trout thing. No one now can really remember Aalto's words, only the style and waggish, seductive ambiguity of the presentation, charm just surviving glamor. Gehry uses phrases like being "rocked in his socks," phrases that would get cheap laughter for a stand-up comedian, but get the applausometer rising at the Zittele in Venice. Nouvel speaks of architecture as "petrified culture." Herzog speaks of the "ordinary" in architecture. Ito speaks of "the shape-no-shape." Zumthor speaks of "thinking within Thinking Architecture." Without strong architecture, realized visions, tacit contracts, and not a little magic, these would all be cognitive delusions reinforcing Solà-Morales's assessment: "The object is no longer to render apparent the practical reality of the building, its justification as form is based on appeals to the deep structures of our psyche, evoking these by means of archetypal images in a way that is as powerful as it is anterior to any logical or narrative discourse."[5] And when you think that chance insight and a certain wisdom arrives, you can be deluded. Gehry begins to propound on his "postmodernist, decon friends," announcing that he just decided to go back, "further than temples to the fish." There is a brief pause and Gehry throws out, timed to perfection, the words "I suppose."

Architecture, I suppose! And suddenly there is a bigger gap than we imagined between architecture and the outside world, between architecture and the language used about it, between architectural conceit, cognitive delusions, and the practical realities that always fall short of magic.[6] Yet this gap is not all fashionable "nonsense" and "undecidability." It is also a condition shared by those architects who can seriously afford to let language go on vacation. A sensuous pragmatism, lost to compromise too easily, is redefined by some as a conceptualism or a contextualism. This contextualism is taken as a description of an attack on the architectural problem from all aspects of its site and consequence, geopolitical, cultural, and social. No systematic models are brought along, adapted, stylized. Nouvel is right when he says that every project needs to be "conceptualized," whether some try to oppose this with a form of a priori tectonism or not. But pragmatism is a game played in the mirror of its own rules. Gehry is as pragmatic when speaking about architecture as Bogart is about "dames." The slap in the mouth would be merely ambiguous if it weren't for the fact that Gehry has designed at Bilbao a museum that looks as if holographic vision has given over to Hollywood vision. Using another language that the adults might despise but the students begin understanding, Gehry bypasses William Gibson and goes straight back to Ray Bradbury![7]

Advertisements used to speak of the "camera with brains." Now they talk of "advanced photo systems." Like architecture, the democracy of photography has been taken over by the mechanical and commercial reproduction of images carnivalized through advertising. It was during the 1980s that architecture collided with advertising as an early form of performance art: I pay, I display. Electronically augmented moments can now be caught by the instant zoom-focus apparatus and become architectural screens. Pressing a button takes literally less than an instant. Perhaps the only innocence left in photography looks like being the state of not owning a camera. Where indeed are the untaken, the unposed, the unrealized, undeveloped pictures? Where is the unarranged photography of architecture's history? With less talk about innocence today in all arts, we are left with the obvious: if nothing can be done straight, then even in photography everything is echo and resonance. Is this a fossilized irony? Jean Baudrillard interprets this as nothing more than an advertising-style irony currently engulfing the world of art.

Results often parody culture itself. All photography looks as if it could become about all other photography. All architecture by photographic reproduction and circulation looks as if it has no other option but to become about all other architecture. And if not, more sophisticated "photoshop" software will ensure permanent manipulation. Yet our innocence about communication seems to increase. How can architecture be read from the hierarchy the architect gives it? And why should it? How, some ask, can a photograph carry all the meanings and interpretation it invites while awarding a hierarchy to those lifted from it?

Problematizing meaning, the architectural bull, departure— no arrival, no a priori signification, antihierarchy—these are all phrases and motives for the more familiar unsteadiness around at present. Without the keys and openness to this unsteadiness, however, each moment will turn itself into a parody of that previous moment, turning the architects' world into a parodist's world. Clearly architects, individually and collectively as a profession, are left with some work to do on communication itself. In his book on language, Rod Mengham tells us how it is the bluntness of Saussure that still needs to be taken onboard: "Writing obscures our view of the language, writing is not a garment, but a disguise."[8] Certainly it is not only the Irish who have a privilege on bulls!

If we are then to watch out for the bull (the rebound in everything) and the bardo (the oscillation from sense to nonsense) what does it ask of contemporary photography? Architectural journals, especially the glossies, have long cataloged other cultures while at the same time producing versions of architecture's invention elsewhere. While we applaud the care with which detail becomes pathological, photography itself threatens not a democracy but a mobbocracy of the image. To speak of the redundant and essential use of photography or film informing and interfering with architecture creates no real oddness today in the wake of cyberspace, digitalization and the privatization of space. And many recognize this redundancy not as an undoing but as an unknowing. Architecture, like photography, has shared the same migraine; the democracy of its own sign in flight has seen it weaving in and out of ideological control, desire, and fatigue. Are we born ambiguously but desire to build lucidly?

Two major schemes of thinking and organizing the world in the last century—modernism and Marxism—have left many of us passengers to the seriousness they demanded, the promise they offered, and the looseness we hijacked and probably abused. We shared the migraine. We belonged but often belatedly, confusingly. A crude arrogance saw many entertain a selected unrest, as if it could privilege "uncertainty" and, making the necessary assertions, harness it all for the approved revolution. Many failed just at the point where it was easiest to succeed, for it proved impossible to leapfrog something we could not recognize. "Marxism," to Claude Lévi-Strauss, "seemed to proceed in the same way as geology and psychoanalysis . . . all three showed that understanding consists in the reduction of one type of reality to another."

Architects took part in the same leapfrogging, pawning one reality for another, believing in dramatic intercourse. Architecture saw itself seduced and then reduced from one type of reality to another. At what stage in our innocence and eminence did other disciplines begin to stretch the evidence of architecture, and how does one recognize that privatized sphere where architecture has become the lonely, seductive, and committed reading of one's own life? Is it out of the question to ask what role film, photography, drawing, and language played in this seduction? Can they all be linked to what in reality must be an appetite for something else?

Let us return to the movement that some feel owes most to these interferences and has left that immense legacy of relativism, postmodernism. Can postmodernism be seen, as Fredric Jameson claims, to have at least revived the appetite for, if not the thrill of, architecture? "The appetite for architecture today, (therefore), about which I am on record as agreeing that the postmodern certainly revived, if it did not outright invent it—must in reality be an appetite for something else." What is this appetite for something else? Meaning-full arrest or unrest? Is it this appetite that keeps architecture's satisfaction always provocatively abstract, always at arm's length, always one step, one film, one poststructural theory away? Do we really search for a collective symbolism, a public coding, instead of opting for an ethical reality, and more modest, minor achievements?

Knowingly seduced, the results turn us and our architecture into semiotic ghosts. We became passengers to ourselves in order to desire an architectural index of readable images. And what, if not an intolerable and seductive jargon, has the acclaimed "democratization of sign" led to in architecture? Is there really a deeper transformation, a sort of conceptual agreement between the space architecture comprehends and the one implicit in film, photography, drawing, and language? Any architecture today, we have come to recognize, has to participate within, yet resist, a delirium of intentionality and interpretation. We need not surf nor become navigators to understand

how any building can locate a critical fantasy from which ordinary and extraordinary claims will be made for it. From social
mission to the hot-wired, architecture today aches for a purpose, a continuous present, a spiritual grounding it thought it
once had so unequivocally. At the same time, a grand indifference is caused by the perpetual unrest in critical thinking and
the longing for nostalgic theory. Architecture becomes a holding pattern of this deferral and reluctance.

If it is difficult, however, to make much sense of a grand indifference in contemporary architecture; it may help us to
think this through in terms of the Tibetan concept of the
bardo: *Bardo,* from the Tibetan word (*bar* = "in between"
and *do* = "suspended" or "thrown"), not only means a transi-
tion but it is also a gap between the completion (realized or
not) of one situation and the onset (realized or not) of another.
As a potential opportunity for liberation, if we are to empty
ourselves of untidy meaning and desolate decoding, we are also
to ask ourselves to award more generosity to impermanence.
Taking this clue, the bardo would be that moment when we
can step toward the so-called edge of the precipice without
feeling the loss of the past, without confusing the nostalgia for
the future. Everyday is quite frankly full of interlinked realities,
all meaningful, all potentially also redundant. Similarly, everything, absolutely everything has to count in architecture; this
is the architectural bardo.

There is a redundancy, a useful "uselessness" if you prefer,
in everyday life that reaches to the heart of the architectural
scene. It reaches so far into the politics and sycophancy of
architecture's communities that it may have numbed, for

longer than we like to admit, the very claims made of architecture. Hence the grand indifference we often witness to architecture's greater scheme. Why should this be so after such a heroic century in one discipline like architecture and such a ferocious, turbulent century in another like physics? If scientists see nothing but change, process, and a "chaosmos," architecture has been forced to come to terms with this flux in its own way. Abusing the language and metaphors of the scientists doesn't always make for shallow, nonsensical architecture. But we have seen claims veiled in architecture, as it has been interfered with, tampered with, invaded, penetrated, ruptured, humped, and undone. We think now that we can spot the coded agendas, the blind spots in architecture, yet we classify indifferently, desolately, almost without thinking.

For instance, if we dared speculate on its language as if it still mattered, the Bilbao Guggenheim would be a type of installation in danger of replicating itself by the very myths, software, and access to the drawing itself. "There is no sense in talking of perversion or excess," Solà-Morales writes, "Gehry's work is what it is, and his schemes make no reference to other schemes—different, earlier, or comparable. This is 'installation' architecture down to the deliberate fragility of its materials and deliberate carelessness with which it treats the tectonic, in the total absence of the Vitruvian *firmitas* . . . Each scheme is exhausted in itself, completely on the outside of any normative intention. They do not offer us any method. They do not affirm any absolute truth."[10]

This is the result of the poetics of the scribble we looked at earlier. Bilbao is the *Tristram Shandy* of twentieth-century architecture. Gehry's drawing is shorthand for what is already present in some of his architecture and what can be grafted on, humped on, from the new. Where one unbalances the other, for example, as in some of Botta's work-on-work, we get systematic style alterations, replications overwhelming greater architectural performance. Where it doesn't, "invisibility" can transform unnecessary architecture. Yet "invisibility" is too mundane to describe the architectural vision of Bilbao. Clearly, when recalling the pre-Cad visionary architecture of the twentieth century, Bilbao is both a return and a departure from those visions. It is quite simple and remarkably consistent because it confirms a countersculptural architecture that has been around for much longer than we care to recognize. Though a vision of the future it still might be, its nostalgia and romance are static, even over the shoulder. Compared to this, Nouvel's nostalgia for the future or Ito's shape-no-shape suggest a more contemporary way of working within the gap. These are not architectures from a scribble. Nor are they the *counter-écriture* of a Barthes scribble made architecture.

When Thomas Krens speaks of Gehry's ego, he not only catches the brilliance and contemporary seduction of the twentieth-century architect at the turning point, a figure often loathed and mocked by outsiders. He catches what the drawing signifies without any of us ever being sure of it. Only someone like Gehry, as confident as Bogart, can abandon one scheme after another, pull them continuously apart, reshape and come up with yet another one. However, this isn't as difficult as it seems if the architectural software, like Maya and more recent programs, are anything to go by. It is the shape and morph of things to come. If not already, this is an architectural gambit

Roland Barthes, *Colored Markers* (1971), from *Roland Barthes* by Roland Barthes (New York: Hill and Wang, 1977). Reprinted by permission of Macmillan Ltd. and Michel Salzedo.

likely to become, as in chess terminology, the endgame. To continue our Beckett parallels, we might say that Godot not only refused to turn up but that the endgame is now a permanent state of existence. Cranky Irish existentialism this may be to some, but crankiness shifted to architectural upset needs more than sculptural theater and spectacle. By looking at the innumerable Bilbao Guggenheim drawings and models, it seems that the architect designs many buildings in one go. All of these could be smaller or larger versions of yet another building. Knowing when to stop the building and let another come out will be part of the architect's not inconsiderable talent. It is not a private, mysterious talent, however. This is an old talent; ancient, renaissance, expressionistic. And any desire for control must edge us toward our own edge, toward our own gap!

An architecture beginning with a fragmented vision, a wrapped statement with layers upon layers of material and sculptural unrest, can find and perpetuate its own architectural logic. This is the bull and the bardo at the same time. The scribble achieves this until finally the scribbles differ little from each other, just as the bardo approaches the bull. In this way it is an architecture always able to loan from sculpture. It becomes the blurring of an architecture from all source, discipline, and boundaries, leaving other architectural limit and provisional realities fair game. These will become architectures as hallucinatory as their reality, fulfilling the permanent and the eternal, asking us to return to where we think we have always been comfortable. These will be architectures trailing the philosophical promise we want from them.

We have heard claims for an architecture of ephemeral promise where the response is momentary, insuperably or irresponsibly provisional, whether the point of departure is a Renaissance reference, an image from Deleuze, or chaos theory. We have heard claims for displacement, disintegration, and deconstruction. Strategies of disarticulation and disjunction, disequilibirum and difference, are considered authentic if they underwrite the future. A cynical, *cynical reason* may ultimately double back on itself, finally returning us even further back than Frank Gehry's "fish thing." We get back to the animals themselves: animals do architecture better and deeper, without thinking of death or rebirth.

We also have architectures threatening to follow fiction and the fallen form of language, structuralism hijacked by postructural orphans and leaking into architecture. Exciting and often unarticulated, we still do not quite know what spaces might be offered when architecture persistently coincides with philosophy. We are not sure what experiences are within to house us, if indeed we need to be housed, in this millennium. Even more mysterious and excitingly erratic are those claims for improbable personal architectures. These emerge from, among other sources, a cyberspace menu and a digitalized imagination. These architectures, hyperradically invented, threaten the virtual reality of all previous architecture, if we are to believe the claims. These claims continue to free-fall with a promise of a tomorrow held off, but just around the corner. Used to contemporary numbness, no one ever admits to belonging to utopias if they can appear so readily available.

From *Roget's Thesaurus,* the word *bull* has at least four entries that we are more or less familiar with: *cattle, solecism, decree,* and *formality.* Though we will not lose sight of the others in our attempt to seize the architectural bull, we will concentrate on the solecistic aspect of the bull. To ignore grammar, to violate grammar, to murder the queen's English is secondary to the seduction and power of the bull itself: a self-contradictory proposition, in modern use, an expression containing a manifest contradiction in terms of involving inconsistency unperceived by the speaker. The bull is a (creative) blunder, a

contradiction, according to Samuel Johnson's twofold definition. As Christopher Ricks forces us to concentrate:

One happy habit, pertinent to an oxymoron's being itself etymologi-
cally constituted as an oxymoron, has long been that of explaining a
bull with a bull. To take up the bull in this way, to rally with it, is
to make clear that at least on some occasions—notably when drama-
tized—such foolery may be a wise move.[11]

The wisdom of such foolery as contemporary architecture?
The investment made by architects in the twentieth-century
in and through language was enormous. Most would acknowledge that the desire to hold back one particular architecture
through language to an agenda it doesn't quite perform was
self-evident and self-defeating. Architectural significance, after
all, conforms to whichever group orchestrates this significance
as power, as discourse. California, Cornell, Columbia, or Cal-
cutta! The more words, the more abuse of metaphor, the more
critical language emerges, the more voodoo we seem to get.
Can we accept this growing "bullish" redundancy of the language used about architecture? Can we accept all this representational ambiguity? Can we accept our squatting, waiting to
move on when the time is right?

Meaning, metaphysics, and magic interweave. Architectural
mantras always take us further and further away from the
evidence of the architecture itself while tempting a deferred
nirvana. Recent research, history, and theory on architecture have been suggesting a dual urgency. An ethics of reading
architecture is mooted alongside the politics of participation
within actual architecture. These are not unconnected. An

ethics of reading architecture would naturally turn our attention to the political control of architectural discourse. This is another way of putting the architectural bull: Who are we to want architecture to mean what we can make it mean? and why?

As a paradigm for architectural impetus, for supplementing redundancy and alibi, language, philosophy, and now new science have become the fodder that previously primitive art, mathematics, biology, or landscape offered. Without them, we have been told, architecture as "built meaning" struggles to exist. However, the achievement of the twentieth century and the frauds it might have played on itself by "undoing" offer one serious consequence that we should take onboard: architecture as "built meaning" should struggle to exist. Writing and research have, of course, been incestuous and relentless during this undoing. We are now of course more familiar with the way society and the era alter the hallucinatory significance given to built form. We have learned how changes in architecture occur that appear subject to fashion, but which have a grounding in earlier political and cultural events. We have learned how architecture crosses boundaries and cultures as it struggles for iconic and symbolic weight. A laundromat can be talked up as much as an airport. We have learned how architecture traps itself as it refines its own relevance and seeks the "logic" it needs to attempt communication. We know that the methodology of classification does not, cannot, always keep pace with change.

Historians tell us that the archive doesn't always come first, as it, too, must fight redundancy and rescripted history. The only thing we might say with a bullish certainty: architecture faced with such redundancies is a paradox no longer beyond us. If we listen carefully to Solà-Morales, important because he is both a serious (self-)critic and architect, we might understand why it may be hasty to abandon all hope in the restoration of an ethical order:

It is not only that the sources of our relationship with the world have extended and multiplied. It is also the case that, as they have done so, the ideals of integration, coherence and synthesis that had presided over the artistic production have become patently unattainable. With the disappearance of these ideals, the practice of architecture presents itself as an undertaking that is humble, fragile, a permanent approximation, insuperably provisional."[12]

Many will no doubt still resist this with sophisticated, sa(l)-vaged critical scenarios, but the insuperability or even the irresponsibility of the provisional must become liberatory. The architectural bull must meet the bardo!

Architecture is but one field of activity connected to life-worlds that supposedly should be able to stay away from frivolity, decoration, and even disengagement. Instead, for the reasons we have noted, it is right there in the thick of it. Condemning the photogenic or mediagenic in architectural production is no easy critical task. Tying the photograph to the surface world of decoration and digitalization and the fetish of seduction does not quite conform to easy explication either. We would need to go deeper to understand the illusion, the seduction and altering—as often represented by the photograph—forced on knowledge, meaning, and communication.

What then would we achieve by such a radical claim that architecture has nothing to do with communication? First, we might aim a little lower and rescue architecture from the claims of photography. To consider architecture as an ecstasy, unfound and unfolded, would be to shift the whole experiential potential of architecture. And though we can write the sentences, read the lines, we cannot always hold to the sophistication of such ideas when the language runs away at every opportunity. Is this but one more definition of the architectural bull that opens us up to the obvious task, to free architecture from the metaphysical claims it cannot uphold? "Freed from God," Alain Finkielkraut puts it, "the thinking subject became the basis of his world and the source of human values."[13] Call it the impossible, call it the unreachable, but this would take us into the future and the past at the same time. We would return to a time when buildings were not necessarily photogenic, to a time when the seduction of images was less understood, less open to proliferation and consumption, less privileged, less mystic, prerational—an architecture less accessible to the seduction of meaning and magic, to the accessibility of an unambiguous hermeneutics. Is this not what some mean by this continuous desire to reach an architecture beyond style? Must the unlearning also begin? "Today we are trying to spread knowledge everywhere. Who knows if in centuries to come there will not be universities for reestablishing our former ignorance."[14]

To establish our former ignorance in architecture? No doubt this is an urgent pedagogical exercise open to its own dangers. What exactly was expected of the architects' language and images early in the twentieth century? Avoiding provocative abstraction, what did meaning offer in the past if not an unsteady exercise in altering more than architecture, more than the environment? Has it always been the higher "bull" for the lower practice of building? Even after William Morris and John Ruskin, earlier architects were no strangers to stylistic tropes. Some of these architects, to word it in language used today, also left no image unconsumed. Yet the writers, journalists, and critics operated in a different architectural language. Theirs was not, as yet, the language introduced and destabilized by Ferdinand de Saussure, Roman Jakobson, and Viktor Schklovsky. If literary studies at that time had not—again to use the familiar—denarrativized the "gaze" or deconstructed the poetics of architectural conformity, can we be so sure that such an activity might not have been under way in some other form? What allows us this eminence today? What makes up our own sorry wisdom?

Consider the surrealists and the strategies of disarticulation that keep returning under different guises. *Duchamps to ourselves,* architectural explanations seem to be reinvented in order to reinvent architectural promise. This is not to say that photography as a way of speaking about buildings has denigrated an architectural vision. Nor is this to say that film and photography have foreshadowed and provoked the form of visual barbarism some think we have today. But there is certain reward if we could understand just why now we hear so repeatedly and dullingly of a "proliferation of images." Just when was that time when architectural images did not blur into each other?

A simple accessible start to "unlearning" might be made by exploring why the word *image* carries more than it signifies?

What does it mean to refer to an architectural image? Does this compromise the experiential, the evidence of architecture as represented, as felt, as sensed? Why and how do words like *signify* and *legible* become part of the critic's, and then the architect's, vocabulary? If an architect like Zaha Hadid can talk fluently of the way her buildings "fold, become incidents on the site, interweave, fragment, meet transparency and are peeled back and then reveal, layer upon layer, slabette upon slabette, yet another quality of tranparency" what does all this mean to the tectonic, cinematic, and photogenic fiat, to the ideas developing behind her architecture? Does it allow the work to be more appropriately described (using photography) as "sleekly handsome" and "dizzily angled"? Or in the case of her ill-fated Welsh National Opera scheme, dazzlingly modern, angled, and difficult? How does this production of architectural vocabulary translate and transform back into the blind spot of architecture?

If language allows us to be more patient with the clear way these "loose" metaphors aid the actual design and tectonic process behind this architecture, why then with some other architects does the jargon reach an intolerable heaviness? And where, if not at the crossroads of semiotic ghosts, does the blind spot lead us? Vitra Fire Station as a film set for a remake of the film *Logan's Run* (according to *Wired* magazine)?[15] And what of interactive and generative architecture or evolutionary buildings? Impossible to photograph or a presupposed modification in the descriptive character of the architecture open to the photograph? John Frazer's morpho-genetic processes allow anyone to try their hand at the netscape, at the evolution of a form by reiterations of simple shapes that have influenced things from yacht design to sun control. In "liquid space," this will become commonplace wherever the software is available. The high level of complexity is a given. Ken Yeang's more adaptive architecture is a building-fit exercise that asks what is left of the architect as buildings begin to evolve themselves to controls set, like advanced photo systems, to (un)alterable programs. Is this not another definition of the ever-changing digital dream of the unprejudiced creative process? Surely not a long way from Cedric Price's intelligent buildings or the work "brought to book" by John Hejduk, the closest to both the bardo and the bull practicing over the past two decades.

The bull and the bardo are then contemporary clues, provisional and permanent. Unperceived perhaps by architecture itself, are we forced to attempt some defense for the increasing unrest, for the indifference, for the blunders and (wise?) "befoolery" architecture may be heading toward? We could reword Ricks's bull as a form of linguistic suicide and temper it with the concept of the bardo. It is possible that the architectural bull aims—inadvertently—at the suicidal success of extinguishing—through the use of non-sense and self-cancelation—the sentiment and nostalgia architecture always manages to suggest. At the same time, in this gap, the shock (the bardo), even tyranny of indifference and ignorance will lift architecture free of its clinging, cloying, twentieth-century preconceptions.

A littoral of no small seduction, this is the architectural bull and bardo. The gap between each thought is where the nature of mind is revealed, an intermediate zone that becomes primary. Movement and unrest here indicate a rite of passage allowing architecture to communicate the logic by which the culture defines its present unrest and solitude. All contemporary work, even without the more idiomatic, stylistic moves, is beginning to possess this continual oscillation. Show the drawings to a committee, to the grown-ups, and if they don't see architecture at all they see merely a hat or a hump. Nouvel, Tschumi, Koolhaas, Libeskind, Ito, Eisenman, Alsop, Gehry, Herzog, de Meuron, MVRDV, UN, Zumthor . . . the names agglutinize unstoppable in the oscillation of meme, taste, and fame. Distrust with language and the codes and metaphors so brilliantly applied to architecture will mean a shift in architectural confidence away from the tongue to the drawing. This might go further, even to the computer realization of architecture, as clients themselves will be able to participate in architecture's alteration and modulation. Thomas Krens, the Guggenhiem director, is right. Gehry's confidence in altering architecture is immense. This confidence will also become commonplace, clearly provocative, clearly original, clearly ambiguous![16] And safe?

In the way we look at the logic by which cultures communicate via symbols, pace Edmund Leach, architecture more so than painting, music, and writing can always straddle the domain between this world and that other. Like a cemetery, we usually pass through this "other world" in transit until our time is up. The realization of architecture from departure to production always allows this movement. To take up where Leach's little Euler diagram left off in anthropology, it is useful to see some of the best contemporary thinkers in the profession continually seeking to put architecture not in a no man's land, but in-between, in a liminal space.

There is reason to rejoice at this. Far from the apocalyptic loss of meaning and direction, confusion and unrest, this is the wonderful redundancy about the present condition. It is architecture's own Himalayan experience, "on having no head!" It is a condition we should at least be grateful that the last century has brought us to. If we are eminent and fragile, architecture is still ours to be eminent and fragile about. It is still ours to make of what redundant mastery we can, together with others in the social production of architecture. Before political control becomes the blind and all-powerful machine that ignores us and creates the environments that we warned ourselves about.

Let us not mistake it, the public is aware of the theater of expected architectural images. Encouraged by classifications of architects and styles, by journals and newspapers, up until recently this theater of recognizable images and architecture was considered the "authentic" architecture made out of the world's undoing. This was the correctness and authenticity by which error and deviation were defined. It is now less and less clear. This authenticity has not always resulted in genuine thrill; sometimes it has produced poor narratives, a failing magic and little resonance of the original work. There has been much polish, transparency, and right-thinking about. Some architecture even unanswers serious redundant issue and expands "spectacle" beyond the pixel, even beyond the limits of the architectural question. It is this theater of form, this expected repertoire of world images, that looked until recently unstoppable. An upset was overdue. The undoing was already prepared in other disciplines besides architecture. Venturi might have been dismissed for his earlier oscillations, but is there not here an accurate warning about the thinness of dazzle, "justifying a conceptualization, a dematerialisation, of architecture via pompous-esoterica transformations of theory, inapplicable inanities questionably borrowed from other disciplines"?[17]

It is, of course, relatively easy to write like this. Even such events as weekend symposiums and world seminars, the discussions and the cocktails, must acknowledge the redundancy of the very moment and must acknowledge the reality outside language. Again, like those hoards of apparently meaningless genes that make up our body, we need such moments so desperately. The day after Gehry put his tongue away at the Zettele, I visited the Guggenheim's collection of the incredible range of models, studies, and drawings for the Bilbao Museum. Did the possibility that we could be astonished not only by scale but by a confirmed vision and space return? It's too early to say. Instead I found myself thinking of these mouths that move in and out when speaking about architecture, culture, art, technology, society, and biscuits. Brodsky catches this oscillation perfectly: "There is something in me, *I suppose,* that always respects the physical side of human utterance, regardless of the context; the very movement of someone's lips is more essential than what moves them."[18]

Regardless of the context? Architecture? Are we moved by Gehry's Bilbao museum or moved about and within the museum? In Venice I sensed that the mutual understanding in architecture was long since celebrated. Understanding was back, much further back than temples and the "fish thing."

Architects can now sit there knowing that the architectural bull and bardo are way back with the ancients but will come, like Mr. Godot, the day after tomorrow.

So much traffic in Heidegger, Derrida, and Deleuze, one wonders if there is anything left to inhabit but a shattered, fragmented dwelling of dazzled language itself. When talking about language and architecture, it is only when we stutter—in our own language or even another— that we feel at home. But where are we at home if not in the language that houses a fragile architecture? The British pluralist D. E. Harding wrote that small treatise, now turned into a thesis on Zen obviousness, called *On Having No Head*.[19] Nothing would be more wonderful than an architecture having no head, without cause, provisional and rigorous but definitely not present. This concerns eminence, randomness, and fragility.

Clarity begins at home, "always the bull strikes awe, even if only at its own fatuity!"[20] Have we come full circle? Now that we know how architecture got its hump, is it time to get off the train, exit the Underground? The clue is ours, and like a good detective story, we need all the clues necessary. The loveliest and saddest landscape in the world is where the Little Prince appeared on Earth and disappeared, just as one day, flying, the writer Antoine St. Éxupéry disappeared, never to be seen again.

Round up the usual suspects! Seize the bull and the bardo! One cannot help thinking of the architects' dilemma as Bogart in *The Maltese Falcon* walks in a tolerable straight line—not a cabbage planter's line, not a critic's line, not a historian's line, but our own line. You don't have to have confidence in me, Bogart says, it's me who has to have confidence in you.

Ditto: Architecture? And just what was Laurence Sterne's precise line? "I did not look closely. I drew a line, no, I did not
even draw a line, and I wrote, Soon I shall be quite dead at
last, and so on, without even going on to the next page, which
was blank."

The architectural bull and bardo. No pulling back from
death? On the contrary, as in the Tibetan tradition, those liberated at the moment of death are considered to be liberated in
this lifetime, not in another, not in one of the bardo states
after death. Now!

notes

Introduction

1. Samuel Beckett, Malone Dies, cf. Originally published, 1902. Ricks, *Beckett's Dying Words,* p. 201.
2. John Hejduk, "Architecture and the Pathognomic," *Architecture + urbanism,* (Tokyo), March 1991. I am grateful to Kirsi Leiman for bringing this to my attention during one of our discussions.
3. Cf. Susan Blackmore, *The Meme Machine* (Oxford: Oxford University Press, 1999).

Chapter 1

1. J. G. Ballard, *High Rise* (London: Panther, 1977), p. 8.
2. This usually gets carnivalized quickly and makes its appearance in the fashion trend journals. See, for example, *Eventful,*

"Herman Werkerk's Architecture Puts Fashion in Space." See also "What Is Modern?," *Dutch* 18 (1998): 103–105. The copy puns, as it does in *Wallpaper,* which has set a pattern for hyping text, ensuring that just about anything can be redescribed to fit the momentary chicness of international ennui and knowingness. This is an indifference in another form, awaiting a serious study of architectural memetics.

3. Jacques Derrida, "52 Aphorisms for a Foreword," in Andreas Papadakis, Catherine Cooke, and Andrew Benjamin, eds., *Deconstruction Omnibus* (New York: Wiley, 1989), pp. 67–69.

4. Le Corbusier's statement in ANY 5 was a paraphrase and differs in translation from that in Beatriz Colomina's *Privacy and Publicity* (Cambridge, Mass.: MIT Press, 1994), p. 6: "Arab architecture gives us a precious lesson. It is appreciated by walking, on foot; it is by walking, by moving, that one sees the order of the architecture developing. It is a principle contrary to that of baroque architecture, which is conceived on paper, around a fixed theoretical point. I prefer the lesson of Arab architecture. In this house, it's a question of a real architectural promenade, offering constantly changing views, expected, sometimes astonishing." Colomina's book provides adequate parallel insight into our themes and is "minding the gap" in another way: "The point of view of modern architecture is never fixed, as in baroque architecture, or as in the mode of vision of the camera obscura, but always in motion, as in film or in the city." No image arrested then? No stop to any arrival in contemporary architecture? See Colomina, *Privacy and Publicity,* pp. 72–73, 312, 329, 376 for further connections to our theme.

5. Ignasi de Solà-Morales, *Differences: Topographies of Contemporary Architecture* (Cambridge, Mass.: MIT Press, 1996).

6. Taken from Iain Chambers, *Identity, Migrancy, Culture* (London: Methuen, 1994), p. 68. We get a fair indication of this oscillating jargon of "heterogenesis" from Guattari to Gaia. What could be more appropriate than language to smear and qualify achievement: "The boundaries of the liberal consensus of its centred sense of language, being, position and politics are breached and scattered as all our histories come to be rewritten in the contentious language of what has tended to become the privileged 'topos' of the modern world: the contemporary metropolis" (p. 14). It is not that I do not know what the writer means. More alarming is that at some time over the last thirty years so many of us have attempted to write something like that. And now? On such language abuse, see Alan Sokal and Jean Bricmont, *Fashionable Nonsense* (London: Picador, 1999).

7. See Bernard Tschumi, *The Manhattan Transcripts, Academy 1981 and Architecture and Disjunction* (Cambridge, Mass.: MIT Press, 1994), and *Event-Cities* (Cambridge, Mass.: MIT Press, 1995).

8. Hejduk, "Architecture and the Pathognomic."

9. *Drawings by Film Directors,* from an introduction by Stephen Frears. New York: Redstone Publishers, 1994.

10. Lyotard's work here would be more relevant than Charles Jencks's indefatigable structuralizing of architectural intent and expectation. It would also be due a timely reassessment after architectural plundering for errant, loose applications in the late 1980s and predictable ennui in the 1990s. See, for example, J-F. Lyotard, *The Postmodern Condition,* (Minneapolis: University of Minnesota Press, 1984), especially Lyotard's *The Pragmatics of Narrative Knowledge,* chapter 6, p. 18.

11. Paul Auster, *The Music of Chance* (London: Faber, 1990), p. 215. Also, for more guidelines on the interplay between film and architecture and the dangers in such an interplay, the reader is referred to a forthcoming study by Antti Ahlava plus "Architecture and Film," *Architectural Design,* 64, 11/12 (1994); François Penz and Maureen Thomas, eds., *Cinema and Architecture* (London, British Film Institute, 1997); Dietrich Neumann, ed., *Film Architecture: Set Designs from* Metropolis *to* Blade Runner (Munich: Prestel, 1996).

12. It would be as well here to attend to Papadakis et al., eds., *Deconstruction Omnibus.* See Geoff Bennington's various texts on this, including "Deconstruction is not what you think," pp. 86–87.

13. See the essay by Joan Ockman, "8 Takes on Jacques Tati's Playtime," *ANY* (Architecture New York) 12, 1995, where she analyzes film's pull on architecture through Tati's awkward brilliance. Ockman also indicates just where innovative analysis might go if released from conventional film and architecture's analogical strategies. The insights are instructive and the reference is impressive. Consult also for other critical texts with some relevance to architecture and film.

14. Douglas Rushkoff, *Cyberia: Life in the Trenches of Hyperspace* (New York: HarperCollins, 1984).

15. See Solà-Morales, "From Autonomy to Untimeliness," *Differences,* pp. 73–90, for an accurate view of this slippage from structuralism into architecture and then on to postructuralism.

16. Frank Heron, *The Upset of the Cerebral,* London: Sisyphus, 1998, pp. 56–75.

17. Heron continues: "The most innovative buildings have become inextricably tied with technological advance and hallucination. They further use the ambiguity of the symbolic, ontic and ontological codes. Solid state, micro-chip fidgetry enhance the skull not the environment!" (p. 72).

18. Charles Jencks, *Architecture of the Jumping Universe* (London: Academy, 1995).

19. See Sokal and Bricmont, *Fashionable Nonsense*, pp. 164–165 and 182–211.

20. The "literal," of course, has a critical history, but we choose to return to it here in conscious echo of its legacy from Alan Colquhoun in 1962 and Colin Rowe and Robert Slutzky's text "Transparency: Literal and Phenomenal" (1956): "To the immediacy of the literal signification they opposed the mediation of an entire linguistic system, by virtue of which such typically rhetorical devices as metaphor, redundancy, and eurythmics entered into architectural play." Solà-Morales, *Differences,* p. 123.

21. For such scenographic concerns see, Helmut Weihsmann, *Gebaue Illusionen: Architektur in Film* (Vienna: Promedia, 1988); Juan Antonio Ramírez, *La Arquitectura en el Cine: Hollywood, La Edad de Oro* (Madrid, Hermann Blunes, 1986). I am indebted to Ahlava for these sources.

22. Seymour Chatman, *Antonioni and the Surface of the World* (Berkeley, Los Angeles: University of California Press, 1985). See also David Mamet's book: *On Directing Film* (London: Faber, 1991), especially for the story "In the Cut" and the notion of uninflection. For a critical interpretation and extension of this in architecture, see my essay on the work of Arrak, "Uninflection and Stubborn Architecture," *Tracing Architecture,* London: Architectural Design no. 132, pp. 39–43.

23. The story is nowhere better told when Venturi speaks on Venturi than in *Iconography and Electronics* (Cambridge,

Mass.: MIT Press, 1996). The useful confusion between scene and screen that Venturi operated within is somewhat turned back on itself as it attempts to describe the journey from signs to scenes, electrographics to electronics, decorated sheds to ducks. How far the moving pixel permit changing imagery and graphics for a multicultural ethos in an information age does not alter Venturi's "literalness," but it does coincide with a gentrification toward Walt Disney. In Europe, it is often hard to apply the same weight to Disney as it is to the Cannonized strip. But I suspect Venturi's brave attempt to locate himself within an electronic architecture is already being rescripted by skateboarders with screens in their machines. See *Las Vegas after Its Classic Age,* Venturi, Iconography and Electronics, pp. 123–128.

24. Venturi, *Iconography and Electronics,* p. 228.

25. It would be critically fair to trace this back to the influence of Archigram, SITE, and Venturi's own work for Best and Basco. For an early trace of this screen work, see Venturi's Hall of Fame competition in New Brunswick, Canada, 1967.

26. Solà-Morales, "Differences and Limit," in *Differences,* pp. 107–116. The writer is referring to other work besides the laconicism of Herzog and de Meuron: the reductionism of Souto de Mura or Juan Nevarro Baldeweg, the controlled gestural expression of Garces y Soria, and the strict monumentality of Francesco Venezia and Roberto Collova. Our concern with the modern media and film remain here with Herzog and de Meuron. Could not the film *Diva* have been the source for the proposed remodeled Tate Gallery in London? And if not, why not? See "Tate Frames Architecture," *ANY* 13:52–59, for an interview with Herzog and de

Meuron, and Sanford Kwinter, "Playboys of the Western World, pp. 60–61.

27. Jacques Herzog in "Beyond Architecture: The Hitchcockian Architecture of Herzog and de Meuron," *Blueprint* (March 1995), ANY (Architecture New York): 26–30.

28. Taken from Stan Allen, "Le Corbusier and Modernist Movement," *ANY* (March/April 1994), p. 42.

29. "Montage—the cutting or the assembly—has become the central operation for both filmic and architectural production . . . The project is a complex document that describes the actions to be carried out by each of the agents who will intervene in the building." Solà-Morales, *Differences,* p. 135.

30. Mamet, *On Directing Film.*

31. Ibid. p. 28.

32. Venturi, *Iconography and Electronics,* p. 15.

33. Gilles Deleuze, *Cinema 1. The Movement-Image* (Athlone, 1986).

34. Solà-Morales, *Differences,* p. 102; also with reference to dance and Deleuze's "folds of a single reality," p. 68.

35. *Dutch,* 18 (1998): 48. See note 2.

36. A phrase originally used by Hugh Kenner.

37. Ricks, *Beckett's Dying Words* (Oxford: Oxford University Press, 1995), p. 155.

38. Jean Baudrillard, *The Illusion of the End* (Polity Press, 1994), p. 19.

39. Paul Virilio, *Lost Dimension* (New York: Semiotext(e), 1991).

40. See Daniel Libeskind, "Radix-Matrix," *Architecture and Writings* (Munich, New York: Prestel, 1997). Not the point of no return for architecture but the *points* of no return.

41. Ricks, *Beckett's Dying Words,* p. 158.

42. See John Hejduk's *Chronotope,* K. Michael Hays, ed., (Princeton Architectural Press, Canadian Centre for Architecture, 1996); also Solà-Morales, *Differences,* pp. 78, 83, for notes on Hejduk. I think Hejduk's architectures in the plural-impossible would be suited to Mamet's lines: "Basically, the perfect movie doesn't have any dialogue. So you should be striving to make a silent movie." Mamet, *On Directing Film,* p. 72.

43. See Fernando Pessoa, *The Book of Disquiet* (London Quartet, 1990), and *Always Astonished* (San Francisco: City Lights, 1988). For more on an interrupted dream of architecture, see Marco Frascari, "The Silent Architect and the Unutterable Nature of Architecture," *The Culture of Silence* (Texas A&M University, 1998), Quantrill and Webb, eds., pp. 67–93, and *Polyphilo,* A. Pérez-Gomez (Cambridge, Mass.: MIT Press, 1992).

44. Solà-Morales, *Differences,* p. 26: "Drawing one of the many possible relief maps of this empty territory in which architecture finds itself makes public and collective a situation that demands to be lived as something individual and private."

Chapter 2

1. Samuel Johnson, letter to John Taylor, Ricks, *Beckett's Dying Words,* p. 161.

2. László Moholy-Nagy, cited in Susan Sontag, *On Photography* (London: Penguin, 1979), p. 203.

3. John Berger, *About Looking* (London: Writers and Readers Publishing, 1980).

4. Roland Barthes, *Camera Lucida, Reflections on Photography* (New York: Hill and Wang, 1981). Dust cover blurb on hardback edition.

5. As an example of this publishing phenomenon, take Konstig (the Swedish art and media distributor). Their *Photography 2* catalog (1997) is a dense sixty-two pages. Divisions indicate photography's appeal and genre limit: "New Monographs," "New General," "Magazines," "General," "Monograph . . . Shopping Bag" (back list). In all the titles, though, there are landscape and environmental concerns. No mention is made anywhere of architecture or buildings as a serious genre in photography.

6. Sontag, *On Photography*, p. 148.

7. Colomina, *Privacy and Publicity* (Cambridge, Mass.: MIT Press, 1994), p. 12. Colomina's book is essential reading for the not-so-fleeting alterations photography offered architecture. For further themes, see p. 8, Barthes; pp. 12–13, Benjamin; p. 31, the problematic status of photography; pp. 42–47, Adolf Loos and photography—turning architecture into a news item; p. 64, architecture "looking good"; p. 100, polysemy; p. 101, disappointed by photographs; p. 104, ineffectivity in magazine; p. 107, Adorno and Jameson; p. 128, contiguity and equivalence within mass media; p. 220, fundamentally contaminated; p. 244, the traveling gaze; p. 250, architecture is not; p. 270, tactile/optical dualities; p. 314, photo opportunities; p. 349, Ruskin purchasing a photograph.

8. Ibid, p. 31.

9. A useful cross-commentary to our discussion is served by Benjamin's original essay, "The Work of Art in the Age of Mechanical Reproduction" and Solà-Morales's "The Work of Architecture in the Age of Reproduction," *Differences*, pp. 133–137.

10. Hélène Binet, interview by Jane Richards, *Light in Architecture* (London: Architectural Design, 1997), pp. vii–ix.

11. Colomina, *Privacy and Publicity,* p. 47.

12. Miroslav Holub, *The Rampage* (London: Faber, 1997), pp. 3–4.

13. See Colomina's analysis of Le Corbusier's own tampering, image modifying, and framing in Colomina *Privacy and Publicity,* p. 124.

14. Sontag, *On Photography,* pp. 12, 22.

15. Mamet, *On Directing,* p. 14.

16. Sontag, *On Photography,* p. 12.

17. Barthes, *Camera Lucida,* p. 36.

18. Ibid., p. 111.

19. Jorge Semprun, *Literature or Life* (New York: Viking, 1997), p. 211.

20. William Gibson, "The Gernsback Continuum," *Burning Chrome* (Ace, 1987), p. 26.

21. Ada Louise Huxtable, "The New Architecture," *New York Review of Books,* June 1994.

22. Fredric Jameson, "Postmodernism and the City," in *Postmodernism, or, the Cultural Logic of Late Capitalism,* (London: Verso, 1992). We refer to the whole essay, especially pages 97–113.

23. Joseph Brodsky, *Watermark* (London: Hamish Hamilton, 1993), pp. 17–18.

24. Euan Ferguson, "Millennium Visionaries Line Up an Experience out of This World," *Observer,* July 28, 1996.

25. Ricks on *Endgame, Beckett's Dying Words,* p. 169.

26. Michel de Montaigne, *Essays* (London: Penguin Classics, 1958), p. 80.

Chapter 3

1. Anthony Storr, *Solitude: The Return to the Self* (New York, Ballantine, 1988), p. 76.

2. Rod Mengham, *Language* (London: Fontana, 1995), p. 50. I continue to consider Mengham's insights some clue to the tragic aspects of architecture and its battles of representational propriety through language games.

3. Laurence Sterne, *The Life and Opinions of Tristram Shandy, Gentleman* (London: Dent, 1967), ch. 40, p. 347.

4. Heinrich Klotz, ed., "Drawing Twentieth-Century Architecture," *Drawing into Architecture, Architectural Design,* (London: Academy 1989). The essay has, however, nothing to do with drawing but is accompanied by drawings from the world architectural theater. Klotz's phrases are referred to in this "mapping" of twentieth-century movements using Sterne's diagram.

5. One should also recall the early decoders: "The theoretical discourse of a Venturi or a Colin Rowe rests, for complexity or for collage, as much on the solidity of established codes as on their coexistence in a world of social communication in which no one can claim exclusive rights to a given language. Out of their tolerance, with their sense of the efficacy of the political economy of the great majority, they accept and promote a discursive system that is rich, various, and multiple, but ultimately transparent, decodable, transmissable, and truthful" in Solà-Morales, *Differences,* p. 85.

6. Cf. Charles Jencks, "What Is Post-Modernism?" *The Post-Modern Information World and the Rise of the Cognitariat* (London: Academy, 1986), pp. 43–56.

7. Cf. Charles Jencks, *The Architecture of the Jumping Universe* (London: Academy, 1995). Interestingly enough, on the book cover Peter Eisenman summarizes Jencks's achievement: "Charles Jencks has the uncanny capacity to announce a new movement in architecture before it has begun. With Postmodernism he was looking at the past. Now, for the first time, with his new book on morphogenesis he is looking at the future. There is no question that his argument will have an important critical effect on architecture at the beginning of the millennium." To be fair, Jencks reads the "gap" in other disciplines just one step before architecture believes it has a mission and purpose and can make more sense of our contemporary existence than other disciplines. This parasitical critical scheming has nothing to do with the creative redundancy we are speaking about here.

8. Helene Lipstadt, "Architecture and Its Image: Notes towards a Definition of Architectural Publication," cf. *Drawing into Architecture,* ed., Klotz, pp. 13–23.

9. Edward Robbins, "The Social Uses of Drawing," *Why Architects Draw* (Cambridge, Mass.: MIT Press, 1994), p. 46. As a running commentary on this essay, Robbins's volume is invaluable, and also to understand the control over discourse that architects rely on through drawing and the short step to a command over the "social division of labour that governs the production of architecture" (p. 48).

10. Colomina, *Privacy and Publicity,* p. 13. For further references to drawing, see pp. 65, 70, confusion; p. 90, Le Corbusier; pp. 269–270, the ineffective and un/translatability; p. 219, the poster and the fresco.

11. To test this compare Christopher Norris and Andrew Benjamin in *What Is Deconstruction?* (London: Academy, 1988), with Baird's primer on deconstruction, *Deconstruction, A Student Guide* (London: Academy, 1991).

12. Cf. Andrea Kahn, "Representations and Misrepresentations: On Architectural Theory," *Journal of Agricultural Education,* February 1994, pp. 162–168.

13. Rinpoche, *The Tibetan Book of Living and Dying,* p. 104.

14. Ricks, *Beckett's Dying Words,* p. 168.

15. Edward Robbins, *Why Architects Draw* (Cambridge, Mass.: MIT Press, 1997).

16. For an exhaustive and informative analysis of the early drawings through to built form, see Coosje van Bruggen and Frank O. Gehry, *The Guggenheim Museum Bilbao* (New York: Guggenheim Museum Foundation, 1998).

17. Ibid., p. 38.

18. Ibid., pp. 37–38.

19. Storr, *Solitude,* p. 76.

20. See *Roland Barthes* by Roland Barthes. (New York: Hill & Wang, 1977), p. 187.

21. For another reference to the draughtsman's contract, see Marco Frascari, *The Silent Architect and the Unutterable Nature of Architecture,* (College Station: Texas A&M University Press, 1998), p. 76.

22. Reima Pietilä, *Intermediate Zones in Modern Architecture,* Marja-Riita Norri and Roger Connah, eds. (Helsinki: 1984). For more on the picaresque, the controlled accident, and the iterative in Pietilä's morpho-genetic (generative?) sketching and drawing, see Roger Connah, *Writing Architecture* (Cambridge, Mass.: MIT Press, 1989).

23. For example, in Gehry's case, consider the whole sojourn of the "fish thing": "The fish shape got me into moving freely. I learnt how to make a building that was much more plastic, and the first chance at that was the Furniture Museum at Vitra. . . . I started to use those shapes, but now I think the thing is to cut it back and see how little of that you can do and still get a sense of immediacy and movement" in van Bruggen, p. 57.

24. Rainer Maria Rilke, *The Notebooks of Malte Laurids Brigge* (London, Picador, 1987) p. 133. This might reasonably be linked to some of Santayana's ideas in *Reason in Art* (New York, 1905).

25. Michel Foucault, *Death and the labyrinth: The World of Raymond Roussel* (New York: Doubleday and University of California Press 1987), p. 135. See also p. 154.

26. John Ashbery, "The Ice Cream Wars," *Selected Poems* (London: Paladin/Carcanet), 1987. p. 250.

27. Jacques Guillerme, "Notes towards the Definition of Architectural Publication," cited by Helen Lipstadt, *Architecture and Its Image.* pp. 12–23. (*Drawing into Architecture,* Klotz, ed.,).

28. This is a concept that Frank Heron explores at some length in "The Logical Fiction," *The Concept of the Cerebral.* See pages 87–123, "Conceptual Leapfrogging and Hijacking the Coincidental."

29. Rushkoff, *Cyberia,* pp. 45–46. I owe this little rush of blood to Rushkoff's survey of "cyber personalities."

30. For a more serious look at phenomenology's lasting relevance to architecture rather than the fashionable reinterpretations of it, Solà-Morales's *Differences* points the way.

31. Prince Charles's infamous phrase about the Ahrends, Burton, and Koralek project for the extension of the National Gallery in London.

32. Rushkoff, *Cyberia,* p. 109, for this and my reinterpretation of other popcultural access in relation to "hyperspace," etc.

33. Cf. Antoine de St Exupéry, *The Little Prince* (London: Pan Books, 1974). Originally published, 1945.

34. Jean Nouvel, an interview with Jean-Pierre Frigo, Arkhitehtilehti. *The Finnish Architectural Review* 2/3 (1995). Also Solà-Morales: "Just as the film director is not personally responsible for the script, wardrobe, sets, or shots of each sequence, neither does the architect have some specially privileged role in the siting, volume, structure, envelope, or cladding of the project: each forms part of the technical diffraction of the architectonic object; none can or should play a principal or decisive role," *Differences,* pp. 136–137.

35. Lightness, Sterne would say of Tristram Shandy, gentleman, *which is "tired of putting on a face that pretends to understand but in fact understands nothing."*

36. Edmond Jabès, *A Foreigner Carrying in the Crook of His Arm a Tiny Book* (Middletown, Conn.: Wesleyan University Press, 1993), pp. 18–19.

Chapter 4

1. Rinpoche, *The Tibetan Book of Living and Dying,* p. 105.

2. Solà-Morales, *Differences,* p. 74: "The diffusion of the linguistic paradigm had two immediate consequences. The first consisted of understanding any cultural product or process as a language in itself, and as such subject to the interdependence of signifier and signified. And given that everything was language, everything was a process of signification; in short everything was communication."

3. Ricks, *Beckett's Dying Words,* p. 193.

4. Ibid., p. 109. Ricks speaks of Deleuze. Not only in terms of the cold shower has this relevance to the architectural traffic in ideas across disciplines: "Deleuze could not be accused of reducing things to the unproblematic, his being a world in which no one ever exclaims, but things aren't that unsimple."

5. Sterne, *Tristram Shandy,* pp. 453–455.

6. Georges Bataille, *The Impossible* (San Francisco: City Lights, 1991).

7. Plato, "Phaedrus" and Letters 7 and 8 (New York: Penguin, 1975), pp. 96–97. Rod Mengham, *Language.*

8. Milan Kundera, *The Art of the Novel* (London: Faber, 1984).

9. Solà-Morales, *Differences,* pp. 10–11.

10. Heron, *The Upset of the Cerebral,* p. 75. Also see Heron's analysis of V. S. Naipaul's concept of "joke knowledge" and the investigations Naipaul makes from it to create his later work. Heron discusses the way architects generally have refused to acknowledge their previous work except in the way it prompts and leads to cleaning out error in their contemporary work. Heron also suggests this will ultimately prove the downfall of the twentieth-century architect, those who now fill the critical histories.

11. Naipaul, "Joke Knowledge," *The Enigma of Arrival* (New York: Penguin, 1987), p. 253. According to Heron's thesis,

the previous three stages of epistemological raiding are hitch-hiking, hijacking, and leapfrogging (Heron, *The Upset of the Cerebral,* p. 77).

12. Heron, "In the Nakedness of Prattle," *Upset of the Cerebral,* p. 136. Heron cites Maurice Blanchot on Foucault: "And if, in this setting 'outside of itself,' it unveils it own being, the sudden clarity reveals not a folding back but a gap, not a turning back of signs upon themselves but a dispersion" (Michel Foucault and Maurice Blanchot, *Foucault/Blanchot,* trans. Jeffrey Mehlman [Zone Books, 1988], p. 10). In other words, Heron continues, architecture and critical rape—the subject of architecture (what speaks through it and what it speaks about) is less architecture in its positivity than the void architecture takes as its own space when it articulates itself in the nakedness of "its prattle."

13. Louis Althusser, *The Future Lasts a Long Time* (New York: Vintage, 1994).

14. Peter Eisenman, *Datutop: Journal of Architectural Papers,* Tampere, Finland, 1994. Interview with Kari Jormakka. The relevance of Eisenman's exercises into architecture's undoing will need more than the present to excavate significance. Libeskind, Eisenman, and Hejduk have only just begun to insinuate themselves in anything like the manner their works are capable of. The implications of, and the debate on, "weakness" can be followed in Ignasi de Solà-Morales, "Weak Architecture," *Differences,* pp. 57–71, and Gianni Vattimo, *The End of Modernity* (London: Verso, 1991).

15. Martin Jay, *Downcast Eyes* (Chicago: University of Chicago Press, 1994), p. 16.

16. Rinpoche, *The Tibetan Book of Living and Dying,* p. 104.

17. Bataille, *The Impossible,* p. 163.

18. Ricks, *Beckett's Dying Words,* p. 98. Not to formulate, no better fomulation than this line by Ricks.

19. Cf. Kenneth Frampton, "Reflections on the Autonomy of Architecture," *Out of Site,* ed., Diane Ghirado (Seattle: Bay Press, 1991).

20. Witold Gombrowicz, *Diary 1* (Evanston, Ill.: Northwestern University Press, 1988).

21. H. W. Fowler, *Modern English Usage* (London: Oxford University Press, 1926), pp. 307–308.

22. Venturi, *Iconography and Electronics,* p. 263. Venturi continues to blur the thinking of neo-modernists into that of the deconstructivists and is always a good guide to the tamed, thinner versions of an esotericism lifting angle and agony for decorative gain. Within sentences, Venturi is honestly blurring the notions of critical detachment, engagement in architecture, and the politics of needing to be noticed in order to get a commission in the first place. He writes like an architect would defend in ice hockey.

23. For information on the ephemeral, McLuhan, and situationism, see Solà-Morales, *Differences,* pp. 126–127.

24. Baudrillard, *The Illusion of the End,* p. 53.

25. Auster, *The Music of Chance.*

26. St. Exupéry, *The Little Prince.*

27. Edmond Jabès, *A Foreigner Carrying in the Crook of His Arm a Tiny Book* (Middletown, Conn.: Wesleyan University Press, 1993), p. 12. The quotation continues: "We admire or condemn what we retain of a work, that is, what we have drawn from it and made our own. Hence the immense libraries any reader takes with a book. But the book never belongs to one person alone. It only seems to submit to the reader. Being prey to all possible readings it is, (like architecture) finally prey to none."

28. Ricks, *Beckett's Dying Words,* p. 152, a citation from Brewer's *Dictionary of Phrase and Fable* (London: Cassell, 1970).

Chapter 5

1. See Christopher Ricks's chapter in full, "The Irish Bull," in *Beckett's Dying Words.*

2. For a sharp and extremely important critique extending the Deuleuzian concept of repetition and difference, see also Solà-Morales, *Differences,* p. 37: "Repetition as innovation, as a mechanism if liberation, of life and death; repetition as will, as the opposite of the laws of nature; repetition as a new morality; repetition that only attains tension and creativity with the fissures of difference, with disequilibrium."

3. The panel, chaired by Sam Hunter, also included Achille Bonito Oliva, Philip Rylands, Marilyn Zeitlin, and Pontus Hulten.

4. See the critical schemata produced around Aalto in the 1998 centenary of his birth. See my set of essays called *Aaltomania: Readings against Aalto?* (Helsinki: Rakennustieto, 2000).

5. Solà-Morales, *Differences,* p. 20.

6. See Venturi's reading of such conceits more sculptural than architectural in *Iconography and Electronics,* p. 112: "Sculpture by its nature can be relatively expensive; even when it is expensive it is cheap by architectural standards. Meaning combinations of *objets* with contrived connections and tour de force construction are other conceits more sculptural than architectural."

7. Venturi, *Iconography and Electronics,* p. 177: "My esteemed colleague Frank Gehry has designed Disney Hall appropriately for *its* context, as hype-heroic gesture par excellence. . . . his building as sculptural gesture looks good from a distance; our building via the quality of its detail looks good up close—and at eye level. We love Los Angeles as the city of the automobile but let us remain the city of brothers, not angels."

8. Mengham, *Language,* p. 173.

9. For this and other insight into the bardos, see Rinpoche, *The Tibetan Book of Living and Dying,* pp. 11, 102–110.

10. See Solà-Morales, *Differences,* pp. 13–26.

11. Ricks, *Beckett's Dying Words,* p. 199. Of importance, also note p. 156, "recent scatalogical and reprehensively gender-specific, 'bull' from bullshit is no relation."

12. Solà-Morales, *Differences,* p. 78.

13. Alain Finkielkraut, *The Undoing of Thought* (London: Claridge Press, 1987).

14. Ibid., p. 20.

15. See *Wired,* "Architects of Change," July/August 1995, pp. 68–71, and how the magazine graphically reinterprets this work.

16. See also Solà-Morales, *Differences,* p. 89.

17. Venturi, *Iconography and Electronics,* p. 7.

18. Brodsky, *Watermark,* p. 30.

19. D. E. Harding, *On Having No Head. Zen and the Rediscovery of the Obvious* (London: Penguin, 1986).

20. Ricks, *Beckett's Dying Words,* pp. 174–179.

index

Aalto, Alvar, 86, 91, 96
Adorno, Theodor, 5, 36
Advanced photo system, 43, 48, 156, 172
Allen, Woody, 92
Alsop, Will, 98
Althusser, Louis, 128, 142, 143
Antonioni, Michelangelo, 15, 16
Appetite (for architecture), 65, 159. *See also* Jameson, Frederic
Architectural bull, 7, 31, 72, 86–87, 101, 105, 121, 137, 151, 168
Archobabble 109, 111, 133
Aristotle, 142
Ashbery, John, 101
Auster, Paul (*The Music of Chance*), 6, 145

Bachelard, Gaston, 27
Ballard, J. G., 2, 10, 104, 106, 108, 110
Bankhead, Tallulah, 76

index
206

Objective vision, 40, 64. *See also* Moholy-Nagy, Lázló

Paris, Texas (Wenders), 15
Peirce, C. S., 30
Pessoa, Fernando, 17, 33
Photographic blind spot, 55, 61, 161
Piaget, Jean, 93
Pietilä, Reima, 95–99
Pirandello, Luigi, 34
Pooh Bear, 8, 31
Pornography of flight, 22. *See also* Pynchon, Thomas
Portland Building, 79–80. *See also* Graves, Michael
Portzamparc, Christian de, 63–64
Price, Cedric, 177
Prince Charles (HRH The Prince of Wales), 69, 109
Provisional architecture, 10
Pynchon, Thomas, 22, 34

Radical montage, 25, 153, 185n29
Reading architecture, 10, 13, 64, 71, 135, 150, 166
Reading photography, 42, 57
Redundancy, concept of (architectural), xiv, 5, 9–11, 92, 108, 141, 144–146, 158, 166, 175
 pure, 131, 141
 useful, 24, 37, 115, 160 (*see also* Bardo)
Ricks, Christopher, 121, 150, 166, 172. *See also* Bull
Rilke, Rainer Maria, 99
Rinpoche, Sogyal, 25, 86, 111, 120
Robbins, Edward, 82, 88, 190n9
Rogers, Richard, 86